Francis William Cross, John R Hall

Rambles round Old Canterbury

Francis William Cross, John R Hall

Rambles round Old Canterbury

ISBN/EAN: 9783337192273

Printed in Europe, USA, Canada, Australia, Japan

Cover: Foto ©Andreas Hilbeck / pixelio.de

More available books at **www.hansebooks.com**

RAMBLES
ROUND OLD CANTERBURY.

BY

FRANCIS W. CROSS & JOHN R. HALL.

WITH ILLUSTRATIONS.

(Second Edition.)

London: Simpkin, Marshall & Co.
Canterbury: Cross & Jackman and Hal Drury.
1882.

(All Rights Reserved.)

CONTENTS.

CHAP.		PAGE.
I.	The Settlement of AUGUSTINE at Canterbury	1
II.	St. Martin's Church ..	9
III.	The Ruins of St. Pancras' ..	15
IV. to VII.	The Monastery of St. Augustine ..	21
VIII.	The Hospital of St. John	45
IX.	The Hospital of St. Nicholas, Harbledown	51
X.	East Bridge Hospital ..	58
XI.	St. Mildred's Church ..	65
XII.	St. Margaret's, St. George's, St. Mary Magdalen's, and St. Paul's..	72
XIII.	St. Stephen's, Hackington ..	78

CONTENTS CONTINUED.

CHAP.		PAGE.
XIV.	St. Dunstan's Church	85
XV.	Holy Cross, St. Peter's, St. Alphege, St. Mary (Northgate), and other Churches	89
XVI.	The Castle, City Walls, and Gates	95
XVII.	Priories, Nunneries, and Alms Houses in Canterbury ..	104
XVIII.	Thanington and Tonford	113
XIX.	Milton, Horton, and Chartham	122
XX.	Chilham	128
XXI.	Nackington, Bridge, Bishopsbourne ..	134
XXII.	Patricksbourne, Bekesbourne, and Littlebourne ..	139
XXIII.	Fordwich and Sturry	145

ILLUSTRATIONS.

St. Augustine's Gateway	Frontispiece.	
		PAGE.
St. Martin's—The Church ..	(to face)	1
,, Norman Piscina ..	..	1
,, "Bertha's Tomb"		4
,, Roman Coffin Lid ..		7
,, Roman and Saxon Masonry		8
,, The Lich Gate		9
,, The Font ..		12
,, Ancient Stone Cross		14
St. Pancras'—Roman Tiles in Wall ..		15
,, Ruins of the Church		17
St. Augustine's—In the Cloisters	..	21
,, Ruins of the Abbey Church	.. (to face)	25
,, Window in Abbot's Chamber		28
,, Door of N.W. Porch		33
,, Ruins of Ethelbert's Tower..		36
,, Bay of Tudor Wall ..		39
St. John's Hospital—Ancient Font ..		45
,, The Gate House		46

Illustrations Continued.

	PAGE.
St. Nicholas' Hospital—Old Alms-Box	51
,, Norman Doorway	53
East Bridge Hospital—The Doorway ..	58
,, The Pilgrims' Hall	61
St. Mildred's—Roman Masonry ..	65
,, The Church ..	68
,, Old Bench-head	69
St. Stephen's—The West Door ..	78
,, The Church	80
St. Dunstan's—Old St. Dunstan's Place ..	85
,, The Church, N. side	87
The City Walls—A Tower on the Dane John.. ..	95
,, Westgate .. .. (to face)	97
The Castle	100
The Priories—The Grey Friars	105
Thanington and Tonford—A Corbel..	113
,, The Church ..	115
,, The Manor House	118
,, The Tudor Gateway ..	120

NOTE.—The illustrations in this volume are from original sketches made during the present year, or from pen-and-ink copies of photographs which were specially taken by Mr. John Bateman, of Canterbury. The aim has been to illustrate the text rather than to ornament the book.

PREFACE.

ANTERBURY CATHEDRAL is too vast, too rich in art, history, and tradition to be included in this little book. But around that matchless pile, and overshadowed by it, there are monuments which—more venerable than Christ Church itself—are memorials of the earliest English Christianity. Few, however, of the many thousands who, year by year, come to Canterbury from all parts of the world, take more than a passing glance, or bestow more than a passing thought, on these hallowed sites. This partly arises from the fact that, while the Cathedral has been repeatedly described and illustrated, there is no book which the visitor can take as an intelligent guide to the city and the surrounding parishes. He must seek for information in various works which are costly and difficult to obtain, or be satisfied with the few pages of meagre and inaccurate description contained in the local guide books.

The authors of this volume have endeavoured to give a popular account of St. Martin's, St. Pancras, St. Augustine's, and the other principal remains of antiquity in and around the city. They have not

PREFACE.

attempted to write a history; they make no pretence to be learned in archæology; but they have tried to make their story of Old Canterbury interesting and, as far as possible, correct. They have visited again and again the places described, taking notes and sketches on the spot. They have added to their own material more valuable matter taken—fairly they hope—from many separate works, ancient and modern; and they have endeavoured to weave the gathered threads into an original pattern. Their plan has been to describe only those antiquities which still remain, and to describe them as they are. This will explain to the reader many omissions.

In the course of their rambles, the authors have received the greatest courtesy and kindness from all to whom they have applied for information, or for free access to the places visited. They take this opportunity to gratefully acknowledge the kindness and encouragement rendered by many friends.

CORRECTION.—*In page* 116, *3rd line from the bottom, for Henry VI. read Edward VI.*

ST. MARTIN'S CHURCH.

CHAPTER I.

The Settlement of Augustine at Canterbury.

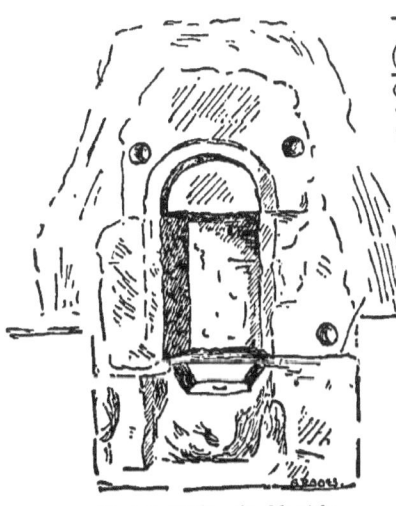

Norman Piscina, St. Martin's.

IN his "Historical Memorials of Canterbury," the late Dean Stanley bids his reader stand "on the hill of the little Church of St. Martin, and look on the view which is there spread before his eyes." Immediately below are the towers of the great Abbey of St. Augustine, where "Christian learning and civilisation first struck root in the Anglo-Saxon race." He reminds us that this spot was the earliest cradle of our most cherished institutions; that "from Canterbury, the first English Christian city —from Kent, the first English Christian kingdom—has by degrees arisen the whole Constitution of Church and State in England." The horizon which bounds our view, as we stand on this hill-side, encloses within its narrow circle the grave of English paganism and the birth-place of English Christianity. Here, first of all, was the voice of prayer and praise heard in the English tongue, uttered by men whose descendants have carried the Gospel to every quarter of the earth. Wherever in the wide world that English tongue is spoken to-day, the little Church of St. Martin's is a known and hallowed spot. To it come travellers from many distant lands, desirous to tread the ground which Augustine trod, to see the ancient sanctuary in which Bertha worshipped, to linger on the spot where the first Englishman was called Christian.

The associations which are enshrined around this spot are a familiar and oft-told tale. But amongst the thousands who tread from year to year these famous sites, there are many who have but the dimmest idea of their matchless interest as relics of the past, and as records of the first dawn of English Christianity. If, on our rambles amid these venerable remains, we can lead any who accompany us to look with deeper interest on the history written in scattered stones and ruined walls, and to set a higher value on the memorials of the past, we shall have gained the end we have in view.

Let us, then, retrace in imagination the ages which separate us from the times of which we write, and suppose ourselves to be standing on this very hill-side about thirteen hundred years ago. The Stour, a higher and wider stream than now, was cutting its channel deeper as it ran swiftly between the wood-covered slopes. Upon its banks stood the wretched cluster of wooden dwellings, roughly built and thatched—some two or three hundred may be—that formed the Canterbury of that day. This was the capital of the most powerful of the Anglo-Saxon Kings of that age—Ethelbert of Kent, the Bretwalda of the English, whose influence was paramount from the southern shore to the border lands of Northumbria. Between the swampy banks of the Stour and the foot of the hill of St. Martin stood his palace, probably a simple group of wooden buildings suited to the fierce fighting-men of a Jutish Court, unused to luxury, and heedless as yet of art.

On the hill-side above the palace there stood the remains of a small church which, according to the Venerable Bede, was "built of old in honour of St. Martin, while the Romans were dwelling in Britain." Bede may have erred in saying this Roman church was built in honour of St. Martin; but it is certain that three or four hundred years earlier than the time of Ethelbert and Augustine, there were Christians at Canterbury among the Roman soldiers and the British people. When Ethelbert's ancestors came into Kent with hordes of hardy Jutlanders the Romans had gone away, and the British Christians were either slaughtered by the new comers, or were driven westward into remoter parts of Britain. At the foot of the hill, and within the precincts of the palace, there stood another Roman building or some remains of one. Whether used in Roman times for Pagan or for Christian worship is doubtful, but in Ethelbert's time it had become a temple, in and around which the King and his people offered their sacrifices, and held their feasts in honour of a god of slaughter and a goddess of lust.

Yet within the circle of Ethelbert's heathen Court the light of the Gospel was not wholly unknown, for Ethelbert's queen was the daughter of Charibert, the Christian King of France. It is probable that most of those who surrounded the Kentish king regarded with hatred and contempt the religion of Queen Bertha, and looked with little favour on the refinement which her Christian practice and gentle life must have brought within the palace. During the many years that the pagan king and Christian queen had been united, Ethelbert must surely have heard the story of the Gospel from Bertha's lips. Her influence, however, had not conquered him; he was still a pagan.

With the coming of Angles and Saxons into the country, if not even earlier than that, the true faith had departed from this little church upon the hill at Canterbury, but when Bertha came to her new home in Kent the ruined building was repaired, and having been dedicated to St. Martin, it became the Queen's Oratory. Bertha had been accompanied from France by Bishop Luidhard, or Liudhard, a retired Bishop, and probably therefore already an aged man, as her Chaplain, and by a retinue of Christian attendants. She must often have had to witness scenes of pagan superstition and heathen revelry, and must gladly have escaped from the heathendom of the palace to the quiet seclusion of St. Martin's Chapel, for prayer and meditation.

Thus, for about a quarter of a century, this little Church of St. Martin remained a Christian oasis in the pagan desert; but the time arrived when the wilderness itself was to blossom. Pagan though he was, Ethelbert must have been a man of noble character, as old Fuller says,—"a good stock fit to be grafted on." The graft prospered, and the fruit which has sprung from it has multiplied and spread over the world.

Stone Coffin at St. Martin's, called "Bertha's Tomb."

While Ethelbert reigned in Kent, there was at Rome a tender-hearted monk whose name was Gregory. He saw, it is said, in the market-place three English youths, fair-haired and blue-eyed, true children of the North. They were a group of slaves, and the sight of them aroused the pity and sympathy of Gregory, who hated slavery. He spoke to the youths, and asked whence they came. He was told they were Angles, from Deira, a Saxon kingdom of Britain. He replied, "It is well, for they have faces of *angels* and should be saved, *de irá*, from the wrath of God, and called to the mercy of Christ." He enquired the name of their King, and was told "Ælla." "Alleluia!" exclaimed Gregory, "the praises of God ought to be sung in that kingdom."

Gregory himself desired to carry the Gospel to the English people. He was not permitted to do so; but a few years later, when he became Pope, he sent into the distant kingdom a band of forty missionary clergy and monks, headed by Augustine, who was Prior of the Monastery of St. Andrew at Rome. They slowly made their way across France, meeting with hardships and difficulties, which led them, being faint-hearted, to desire to turn back, and abandon their mission. Gregory urged and encouraged them to persevere, and at last they landed in the Isle of Thanet. The exact landing place is unknown, but they were bidden to remain at the spot until Ethelbert met them, and heard what they had to say. This interview took place in the open air, in the spring of 597. Augustine set forth the object of his coming, and his words were interpreted to the King. "These are fair words and promises," replied Ethelbert, "but because they are new and uncertain, I cannot at once assent to them." Nevertheless, he gave the strangers permission to enter Canterbury. They came along the Roman road, and down St. Martin's Hill, singing a Gregorian chant as they marched in procession, and bearing aloft a silver cross and a picture of the Saviour. They passed the Church of St. Martin, where Luidhard had ministered until his death, and on reaching the city they first took up their abode at the "Stable-Gate," which was close to the spot on which St. Alphege' Church now stands. Soon afterwards they were permitted to worship at St. Martin's, which they entered chanting "Open ye the gates, that the righteous nation which keepeth the truth may enter in." (Isaiah xxvi.) It was not long ere Ethelbert resolved to accept the new faith. He was baptised by Augustine on Whit-Sunday of that same year (597). It is not improbable that this event, so momentous in its consequences to the English nation, took place at St. Martin's, or in the Stour below. The King's conversion ensured that of his people, and on the Christmas Day following ten thousand of them were baptised in the waters of the Swale.

We have spoken so far of Augustine the missionary monk, but between the conversion of Ethelbert and the baptism of the ten thousand men of Kent, Augustine had gone over into France, and had been consecrated at Arles. He returned as the first Bishop of the English Church, and Canterbury became the seat of the English Primacy. Owing to the influence of Ethelbert the religion of Christ had within a few years been accepted throughout the Anglo-Saxon kingdoms. So far the footsteps of Augustine are traceable in history. In the following century, however, we enter a misty region of tradition, in which facts are uncertain, and the documentary evidence more than doubtful. Bede finished his history of the Church in 731, and he might have gathered his knowledge of the events at Canterbury from those whose span of life extended back to the time when some of Augustine's companions were still in existence.

Bede states that Augustine on his return from France repaired and consecrated an old church which the faithful among the Romans had erected, and that he dedicated it "in the name of God the Saviour and Our Lord Jesus Christ." These words were assumed by the writers of the spurious early charters to refer to the foundation of Christ Church, and it has been generally said that the present Cathedral of Canterbury stands on the site of that which Augustine dedicated. It is doubtful if the words of Bede can fairly be so interpreted. They would rather seem to refer to that Roman church of which the actual foundations have been opened to view quite recently at St. Pancras; the church of which Thorn, a monk of St. Augustine's in the 14th century, wrote:—" There was, not far from the city towards the east, as it were midway between the church of St. Martin and the walls of the city, a temple or idol-house, where King Ethelbert, according to the rites of his tribe, was wont to pray, and with his nobles to sacrifice to his demons and not to God, which temple Augustine purged from the pollutions and filth of the Gentiles, and having broke the image which was in it, changed it into a church, and dedicated it in the name of the martyr St. Pancras, and this was the first church dedicated by St. Augustine."

It is said that Ethelbert, on accepting Christianity, gave up his palace to Augustine, who founded there the monastery which was at first dedicated to St. Peter and St. Paul, and at a later time was re-dedicated to Augustine himself. It is almost certain that in obedience to the orders of Gregory, the pagan groves and temples were not destroyed, but were devoted to the worship of Christ. The conversion of the Kentish people was, no doubt, more a proof of loyalty to their king than a result of Augustine's preaching, or a miracle of grace as it was represented to be. Even Ethelbert's own Christianity was probably, like Constantine's, a mingling of the new faith with the old paganism, and it is recorded that his son and successor went back for a time to his old gods when Ethelbert and Augustine were no more.

It has seemed desirable to give a brief sketch of the history and traditions which gather round this remarkable spot, ere we pass over the entire site, and describe what there remains of the buildings in which Bertha, Ethelbert, and Augustine joined in Christian worship, the foundations on which were laid the whole structure of the English Church.

PIECE OF ROMAN COFFIN—ST. MARTIN'S.

ROMAN TILES AND SAXON MASONRY IN THE SOUTH WALL OF THE CHANCEL OF ST. MARTIN'S CHURCH.

CHAPTER II.

St. Martin's Church.

T. Martin's is the most ancient church in England, and it was at one period the only church in this country in which Christ was worshipped. Within its walls Christian soldiers of the Roman empire and Christian converts among the British might have united in the service of the Saviour. It survived the fall of Roman and Briton, the pillage of Saxon and Dane. The Normans, who pulled down most of the churches, to rebuild them according to their own fashion, spared this, though they left their hand-work upon and within it. It is not a site merely; the fabric is there. The very walls are in part, at least, those which resounded to the praises of God fifteen hundred years ago.

The evidences of Roman material in the walls of St. Martin's are abundant throughout, but while in some portions the Roman tiles are mixed with other material, elsewhere they seem to have been undisturbed since the day when they were laid one upon the other. This is the case especially in the south wall of the chancel, a portion of which has every appearance of being original masonry. Quite recently, Canon Routledge, who has devoted much time to the study of this church, has laid bare the internal wall of the nave on the south side, and has discovered there also original Roman tile work, overlaid with the characteristic salmon coloured plaster; so that it is probable that a considerable part of the walls of the early Romano-British church remain intact. Then there is another part very full of Roman tiles in good condition, but mixed with flints and rough stones laid together irregularly. It is no straining of probability to attribute this portion of the work, in the chancel especially, to the period when the ancient Roman building was repaired in order to fit it for Queen Bertha's sanctuary.

In that part of the south wall of the chancel in which we suppose the masonry to date from Saxon times is a very rudely formed, flat headed arch, composed of three blocks of oolitic stone. It has been spoken of as a leper's window, which does not seem probable. It must have been the work of unskilled masons such as we may suppose Ethelbert's artificers to have been. A short distance east of this rude arch is a small round-headed arch, formed of thin slabs of stone with wide joints of sea-shore mortar. The sides of the arch are composed of Roman tiles very regularly and evenly laid. It has been discovered that the Roman tiles are regularly continued through the wall to the inner surface, and the whole appearance and character of this arched doorway is suggestive of very early construction. The engraving on page 8 gives an accurate illustration of these two interesting arches and of the wall masonry to which we have referred.

It has been supposed that the nave of the present church was wholly an addition to the pre-Norman building, but Canon Routledge's discoveries show that a part of the nave wall is of the Romano-British period. In an old drawing of the church given by Stukeley there is plainly shown a round arch close to the east end of the south wall of the nave. On carefully examining that part of the wall in certain lights the position of the arch can be traced in the flint work facing of the wall. This arch must have been filled up before the construction of the

Norman piscina on the other side of it, within the nave, and it probably belonged to the Saxon if not to the Roman building. At the west end of the same wall is an early English arch filled up and subsequently pierced for a window. This was evidently the arch of a south porch or door. Formerly there was a north porch also, but this too has been removed and the wall filled in.

The plan of the church is of the simplest kind; a west tower opening to the nave, which is divided from a chancel of equal length by an early English arch. There are no aisles, but on the north side of the chancel is a small recess used as a vestry. In one of its windows is an interesting representation of Bishop Luidhard, Queen Bertha's chaplain. The inscription within the nimbus is "Lindardus Episcopus." The Bishop has a crosier and mitre in his hand. This piece of painted glass was, we believe, found some years ago in some old curiosity shop in London. Whatever its origin it is admirably suited for its present position, and it is alike excellent in design and execution. The painted glass of the other windows is all modern. One shows St. Martin parting his cloak with the beggar; another represents Gregory the Great.

The Norman piscina (p. 1), mentioned above, is said to be one of the earliest; the stone-work has been pierced to support a canopy. In the north wall of the chancel is a very perfect aumbry, still having the carved oak door so rarely to be met with in these receptacles for the sacred vessels. It is attributed to the 15th century. In the same wall of the chancel is an arched recess, of modern construction, which contains an ancient stone coffin. There is no inscription or carving upon the lid, which is a slab of oolite, but it is commonly spoken of as "Bertha's tomb" (see p. 4).

In the year 1845 the church was under restoration by the Rector (the late Rev. W. J. Chesshyre), and in the lowering of the chancel floor the coffin was discovered imbedded in the wall. It was opened in the presence of the Rector and of the Hon. Mr. Finch. The lid was removed with considerable difficulty, being firmly cemented on. The inside of the coffin was hollowed to the shape of the body, a cavity being formed for the head. Mr. Chesshyre was strongly of the opinion that the coffin might be that of Queen Bertha, whom a tradition of no great antiquity represented as having been buried in the church. This tradition is mentioned by Fuller (1655), but Somner, in 1640, makes no allusion to it, so that it could scarcely have been current in his time. It has to contend against the distinct assertion of the old chroniclers that Ethelbert was buried beside Queen Bertha, in the *porch of St. Martin*, in the Abbey Church of St. Peter and St. Paul (St. Augustine's Abbey). All that we can say, therefore, is that in the Church of St. Martin is a nameless, ancient coffin which some believe to be that of the gentle and pious Bertha. The Latin inscription, placed by Mr. Chesshyre above the tomb, gives expression to the doubt as to the burial place of Queen Bertha.

Many have been the opinions expressed on the age of the Font, which has probably given rise to more discussion, and been regarded with greater interest than any other font in the kingdom. Some even have declared it to be as old as the time of Ethelbert and Augustine; many have maintained that it is certainly a Saxon font, and others that it is certainly Norman; at last we seem to have arrived at a composition of these two opinions, and archæologists of eminent ability consider that the font itself is Saxon, but the carving upon it Norman. This last theory appears to be one in which the actual evidence and the uncertain tradition can alike be included. The font is made up of three separate circular bands and a rim. The three bands are composed of twenty-four distinct stones. The two lower bands are ornamented with circles irregularly and rudely interlaced. One stone bears what resembles a Runic knot, and it would be difficult to say why the ornaments in the two lower bands should not be pre-Norman. On the upper band is carved a series of interlaced round arches; this is almost certainly Norman. Contrasting the formal pattern of the one with the archaic irregularity of the other bands, we should be inclined to suppose them to be the work of two different periods. Mr. Loftus Brock points out, however, that the whole carving of the font was done with a chisel of not over a quarter of an inch, and appears to have been executed at one time, and that a late Norman date; but he argues, with much force, that as many cases even now occur of old fonts being "decorated" with carving quite out of keeping with the age of the font itself, such might also have been done by the Norman craftsman who chiselled the pattern on this ancient font. The font now stands on a modern base. It was taken to pieces and remade during the restoration of the Church.

Old brasses are rare in Canterbury, and though those in the pavement of St. Martin's are not specially remarkable they are worth mention. There are the figures of Michael Francis Sertivoli, and Jane his wife, with the date 1587. A plate, also in the Chancel pavement, records that " Here lieth Thomas Stoughton, late of Ash, in the County of Kent, gentleman, who departed this life the 12th June, 1591." There is also a plate to Stephen Fulks and Alice his wife, dated 1406, the oldest dated brass in Canterbury. This calls to mind an inscription on an ancient finial cross which was dug up in the year 1767, close to the churchyard. Upon one face it bears Helbwhyte, in raised letters within a hollow moulding. On the other side the words " And Alys ys wyfe," are sunk in the hollow groove showing that it was used as a memorial of some dame Alice at a later period. This old cross now stands on a pedestal close to the Lych Gate and is well worth observing. There is an interesting mention of it in the appendix to Mr. Bryan Faussett's " Inventorium Sepulchrale."

In a letter to his friend, Dr. Ducanel, dated Nov. 13, 1767, he say:—" About ten days ago an ancient stone cross such as you have seen on the gable-heads of churches was discovered in a garden near St. Martin's Church. On one side is exculpt a word which we cannot make out, but is no doubt the name of a man. On the other side is insculpt four words which, like the former, being made up of barbarous monkish letters, of no particular alphabet, puzzled me out of patience; but at length our friend Pearson unravelled them, and they were no more nor less than 'And Alys his wife.' Say nothing; our President is to try if he can make them out."

Cross found at St. Martin's.

A number of coins, with a Roman intaglio and a gold ornament containing coloured glass were dug up at St. Martin's. One of the coins is remarkable both for the beauty of its execution, and as bearing the image of Bishop Luidhard, the Chaplain of Queen Bertha. It has often been figured and described. During the restoration, a mediæval chrismatory, or vessel for the sacred oil, was found in the wall. It is now in the possession of Mrs. Chesshyre of Barton Court.

Many have desired to be laid in a spot so hallowed with Christian memories as St. Martin's. Such was the wish of the late Dean Alford, and there, in the spot he selected, is his grave, under the spreading yew-tree beneath which he often stood to look down upon his own great church. It bears that singularly felicitous inscription he had pencilled down to be carved upon his tomb. "Deversorium viatoris Hierosolymam Proficiscentis." (The sojourning place of the traveller to the heavenly Jerusalem.) Many have vainly sought to discover whence Dean Alford drew this poetical and beautiful figure.

CHAPTER III.

The Ruins of St. Pancras'.

THELBERT'S pagan temple, when reconsecrated to Christ, was dedicated by Augustine to St. Pancras. We may feel sure that it was in St. Martin's that the Italian missionaries first held their Christian services, but it is most likely that St. Pancras' was the church in which Englishmen first bent the knee to the Saviour. Dean Stanley has given an interesting account of its Patron saint :—" Pancrasius " he says "was a Roman boy of noble family, who was martyred under Diocletian at the age of fourteen, and being thus regarded as the Patron saint of children, would naturally be regarded as the Patron saint of the first fruits of the nation which was converted out of regard to the three English children in the market place (of Rome). And secondly, the Monastery of St. Andrew on the Cœlian Hill, which Gregory had founded, and from which Augustine came, was built on the very property which had belonged to the family of St. Pancras."

The church of St. Pancras has long ceased to be more than a ruin, and but a fragment of what remains above ground probably stands as it did in Augustine's time, yet it is a venerable monument, whose broken walls and crumbling arch are built of the materials which were first laid together by Roman or British Christians upon the foundations which, after being buried for so many ages, have again been exposed to view. Modified in form alone they have stood where they now stand while empires have fallen into more complete decay, and the English nation has slowly built itself up.

The church of St. Pancras stood between the Abbey of St. Augustine and the church of St. Martin. It is partly in the grounds of the Kent and Canterbury Hospital, and partly in a field on the property of Mr. Horne, who kindly gave us full liberty to visit and explore it. The ruins above ground include the east wall of the chancel, containing a large and lofty pointed arch, turned in Roman tiles; it was that of the great east window of the mediæval church. Portions of the north and south walls of the chancel are also standing, and are from 2ft. 6in. to 3ft. thick. They are composed of very various materials, but Roman tiles abound in every portion of the structure. On the south side of the chancel, the lowest part of the wall is composed wholly of tiles, quite evenly laid, and this is probably part of the original Roman structure, but in the other portions the Roman bricks are mixed with flint, with rough and with roughly-squared stones. In several places stones showing early Gothic mouldings (the spoils of the destroyed buildings) have been used to repair the fabric. The east wall of the church is joined at right angles by the old boundary wall of the Monastery, which in this place is very thick, but is composed of chalk, rubble and flint, so loosely put together that it has been quite honeycombed by rats.

Within the chancel and in its south wall is part of a piscina, the moulding on one side and a part of the hollowed stone basin remaining. A few feet from this, in the same south wall, is a part of an arched doorway 7ft. wide, and from the arc of the curve remaining, it was apparently a flatly rounded arch turned in Roman brick. It appears to have been more ancient than the surrounding building, and there is no trace of it on the exterior of the wall.

The extremely ancient stone font of St. Pancras, which was found many years since within the ruined chancel, now stands for use as a flower-vase in the garden of a house at the back of the College buildings. It is a rough-hewn square block, with a circular basin chiselled out, quite archaic in character, and without the least trace of ornament.

Ruins of St. Pancras'.

The boundary wall running westward from the church is full of Roman bricks. In this wall is the famous stone which, for how many ages we know not, was firmly believed to show the marks of the Devil's talons. The monks of St. Augustine's were doubtless the authors of the story, which ran that when Augustine first held worship in St. Pancras, "the Devil, all enraged, and not brooking his ejection from the place he had so long enjoyed (as a heathen temple), furiously assaults the Chapel to overturn it; but having more of will than power to actuate the intended mischief, all he could do was to leave the ensigns of his malice, the print of his talons." Somner quotes the tale from Thorn, and adds,—"Let him believe it that can give any credit to it, for me; and so I leave it." He says, however, that "on the walls outside of the south porch such tokens as the historian will have it to be the marks of the Beast are visible enough." The external wall of the south porch is no longer standing, but the graven stone is built into the wall facing the adjoining field.

In the summer of 1881 some excavations which were made in the Hospital field, on the south side of the ruins of the mediæval church, led to the discovery of the foundations of the Roman building which was dedicated by Augustine to St. Pancras. These were opened up under the direction of the Bishop of Dover and Canon Routledge. The latter gentleman ably explained the remains to the Archæological Society, at their Canterbury meeting, in July of the same year, and prepared a ground plan of the entire site of the church. We had already pointed out, in an article on St. Pancras, that the lower part of the south wall of the chancel was wholly composed of Roman tiles regularly laid, and that there stood above ground a considerable piece of wall which had evidently formed part of a Romano-British building. The subsequent discoveries confirm the observations, and, although the foundations have not been laid open on the north side, we can now get a very clear idea of the size and shape of the original building. The foundations of the south wall of the nave and part of the chancel have been opened, as well as those of a west porch, and a south porticus. Starting at the west we commence with the previously mentioned wall, built of Roman tiles, evenly laid, with sea-shore mortar. This wall is from 9 to 10 feet high, and about as long; it is undoubtedly a part of the building in which it is believed that Christians assembled to worship during the period of Roman occupation of Britain, and those very bricks must have resounded to the voice of Augustine as he preached to the Kentish court. This piece of wall formed the north side of the west porch, and thence we trace, in the foundations, the line of wall until we come to a south porch or porticus of the same size (10½ ft. by 9½ ft.) This south porticus is one of the most interesting spots on English soil. It contains the masonry of an altar, which there is reason to suppose stands on the foundations of that before which Ethelbert sacrificed to heathen gods, and which Augustine consecrated to the God of Truth. The monkish chronicler of St. Augustine's, writing in the 14th century, said :—" There is still extant an altar in the southern porticus of the same church, at which the same Augustine was wont to celebrate, where formerly had stood the idol of the king." Five hundred years after Thorn wrote, the porticus and the altar are unearthed, and bring confirmation to his facts, though none to his legends.

Continuing to pass eastward along the foundations we come to the end of the wall of the nave. At this point there is a portion of a large round Roman pillar with its base imbedded in the original masonry. Beyond this the chancel wall of Roman tiles can be traced for some distance. Canon Routledge's plan gives the dimensions of the nave as 42½ by 26 ft., and of the chancel as 31 by 21 ft.

The Roman wall of the south porticus was pierced during the fifteenth century for a new doorway; the floor was covered with tiles probably of the same date. Below them there was a layer of earth, and then a concrete floor. Fragments of Roman pottery and fused bronze were found during the excavations, and the earth showed clear signs of the action of fire. The west porch had also a pavement of mediæval tiles, below which were discovered some remains of very ancient interments. In one case the skeleton, nearly perfect, lay upon the earth, and was covered in with rough stones formed into a rude kind of coffin, above which was a large oolitic slab not unlike that of the stone coffin at St. Martin's. Unfortunately, no articles were discovered to give a clue to the period in which these bodies were buried in the porch of the church. The mouldings of the doorway leading into the church are Norman. The mortar of the Roman walls are in some parts of the salmon coloured tint due to pounded tiles.

It will be seen that these ruins of St. Pancras are of national interest and importance. Unfortunately there is no security that such priceless relics of our earliest history will be cared for or preserved, but an effort should be made to rescue the remains of Augustine's first church from desecration, and secure them for future ages. The county of Kent contains a great number of wealthy churchmen and antiquaries.

Can they not raise a fund to purchase the whole site, to be conveyed to the Warden and Fellows of St. Augustine's, under covenant securing to the public for ever the right to visit and inspect the ruins? These are days in which all intelligent persons deplore the ruthless destruction of ancient monuments which might have withstood the hand of time during centuries yet to come. We no longer expect to see column and arch, and traceried window carted away to decorate some garden wall, or marble tombs hacked to pieces for common building material: our age has revived the love of beauty, and the respect due to the venerable remains of ages whose art-sense was higher and purer than our own. Surely, therefore, St. Pancras', with its fifteen hundred years' history and associations of profound interest to English Christians will be duly appreciated and religiously preserved.

CHAPTER IV.

The Monastery of St. Augustine.

AUGUSTINE received from the hands of the king a grant of land for the erection of a monastery, in which to house the band of missionaries—for as such were they sent hither—and to establish a school in which promising English converts might be trained as priests and preachers. The founder of this earliest monastery in England, "the first born, the first mother" as it was called in Papal bulls, was not a monk of the sort that in later days brought scandal and shame on Christendom. The friend and messenger of the simple and pious Gregory was a monk of poverty, and had little thought of that luxurious and lordly pomp which afterwards became the rule within the Conventual halls. Dr. Hook (Lives of the Archbishops, vol. I) tells us what manner of men they were who now settled down in the Kentish capital : they were indefatigable in preaching the Gospel ; their books were few, but many could repeat large portions of Scripture ; few were they who did not know the Psalms so as to join in the service of the church; the readers were incessantly employed; in the church, at meal times, early in the morning, and late at night, the lector was at his post; they lived in primitive simplicity, and were perfectly contented with what was provided for them. Augustine laid the foundation, but did not live to see the completion of the structure first raised. The date of his death appears to be uncertain; it was probably within seven or eight years from his landing in England, but in that short time much was accomplished. Augustine in bodily stature towered a full head above his companions, but it does not appear that his mental pre-eminence was proportionate to the physical; yet that he was capable of many of the actions ascribed to him ought not to be believed on such unreliable testimony as that of the Anglo-Saxon historians. It would be going beyond our province, however, were we to enter into this debateable land.

Augustine died with his work only fairly begun. His royal convert was beside him in his last moments, and comforted him, we may be sure, with a promise to continue true to the Faith and to its ministers. The remains of the missionary archbishop were buried in that ground which afterwards became so renowned a cemetery, and near the church whose first stone he laid. His successor, Laurentius, completed this abbey church, and dedicated it to St. Peter and St. Paul in the year 613, for it was not till the rededication by Dunstan, in 978, that it also received the name of St. Augustine. Ethelbert was present at the consecration, but his gentle queen had already been laid to rest. Her remains, with those of Luidhard and Augustine, were then removed to the north porch of the church; and three years later the body of Ethelbert, the first Christian Englishman of whom we have record, was also buried in that porch.

Upon the death of the king, a time of trial and adversity came upon the newly-founded church. Ethelbert had married again, and his son Eadbald, having resolved to wed his step-mother, began to quarrel with those who opposed his desire; he turned again to the heathendom which he had but half abandoned. We are told that Laurentius, in his despair, passed the night in the church, and fell asleep, with the thought in his mind of giving up the mission and returning to Rome. In the still midnight hour, St. Peter appeared, and scourged the faint-hearted Archbishop till his back was scarred and bleeding. In the morning, the fresh wounds were exhibited to the King, who was so impressed by the "miracle" that he renounced his unholy intentions, and was baptised. He became a generous patron of the monastery, which rapidly grew greater and richer as the years rolled on.

It was not only at Canterbury that reaction against the new faith had set in. Mellitus, bishop of London, was driven out, and came as a refugee to the monastery. A year after his coming, he was, on the death of Laurentius, consecrated as his successor in the Primacy. A story is told of him which is not quite so legendary as that of Laurentius. He was lying ill with gout when he heard that a great fire was spreading rapidly among the thatched, wooden houses of the city. He was carried to the spot, and, in answer to his prayers, the fire was stayed. This tale is told by Bede, to whom we owe most that is known about Augustine and his successors at Canterbury. Bede obtained his information from the Abbot Albinus, the first abbot who was an Englishman. He was "a man skilled in all kind of learning," and he sent by letter and messenger to the famous monk of Durham whatever knowledge of the early history of the monastery could be gained from the written records, or the oral report of aged brethren. Thorn, the monk of St. Augustine's, wrote at a much later date, and is less to be trusted, being farther removed from the events he described.

As the Church in England, grew older its wealth and power accumulated, but its pristine simplicity was lost. The conventual life became less pure; luxury and revelling desecrated the monastic halls; and bitter jealousies and conflicts arose between the rival establishments of St. Augustine and Christ Church. We read of a sumptuous feast, given by Abbot de Bourne to six thousand guests, and no opportunity was lost of lodging and entertaining kings and nobles within the monastery; the mitred Abbot was jewelled and arrayed in gorgeous robes; he rode forth to chase, or travelled to Parliament with a retinue befitting a monarch; the convent kitchen was enlarged; hosts of retainers were engaged in the service of the great officers; gratified kings bestowed estates upon those who excited their superstition, and ministered to their pleasure; and parish after parish became annexed to the monastery, for provision of food or clothing, within which simple terms the costly luxuries of mediæval monasticism were conveniently included.

In Thorn's time the Abbot of St. Augustine's possessed nearly ten thousand acres of land, and the revenues and rights of at least a dozen great parishes in Kent. The sanctity attaching to a spot in which Augustine and the next nine Archbishops were buried must have added greatly to the influence of the Abbey in days when all men held belief in the miraculous powers of dead saints' bones. The fact that the Christian kings of Kent were interred in the same place would also have its weight, and no chance was lost of adding to the number of saintly relics. Thus Abbot Elstan in 1030 caused the bones of St. Mildred to be brought from Minster to the Abbey. We have the usual legendary tales of the wonderful works wrought by virtue of the relics. According to accounts they were potent in time of fire and flood, and could even stay the still more terrible scourge of Danish ferocity. It was in 1011 that the Danes assailed and sacked the city of Canterbury and destroyed the Cathedral. They seem to have spared St. Augustine's. The Anglo-Saxon Chronicle says that Abbot Elmer betrayed the city to save himself and his monastery, but of course the monks tell another tale. Thorn's account is that when the ravaging Danes entered the monastery to carry away what they could lay hands upon—"one of them more desperately wicked than the rest of his comrades, comes boldly to the sepulchre of our Apostle St. Augustine, where he lay entombed, and stole away the pall with which the tomb of the saint was covered, and hid it under his arm. But divine vengeance immediately seized upon the sacrilegious person, and the pall which was hid under his arm stuck to the arm of the thief, and grew to it, as if it had been new natural flesh, insomuch as it could not be taken away by force or art, until the thief came and discovered what he had done, and confessed his fault before the saint and the monks, and then begged their pardon. The example of divine vengeance so affrighted the multitude of the rest of the Danes, that they not only offered no violence to this monastery

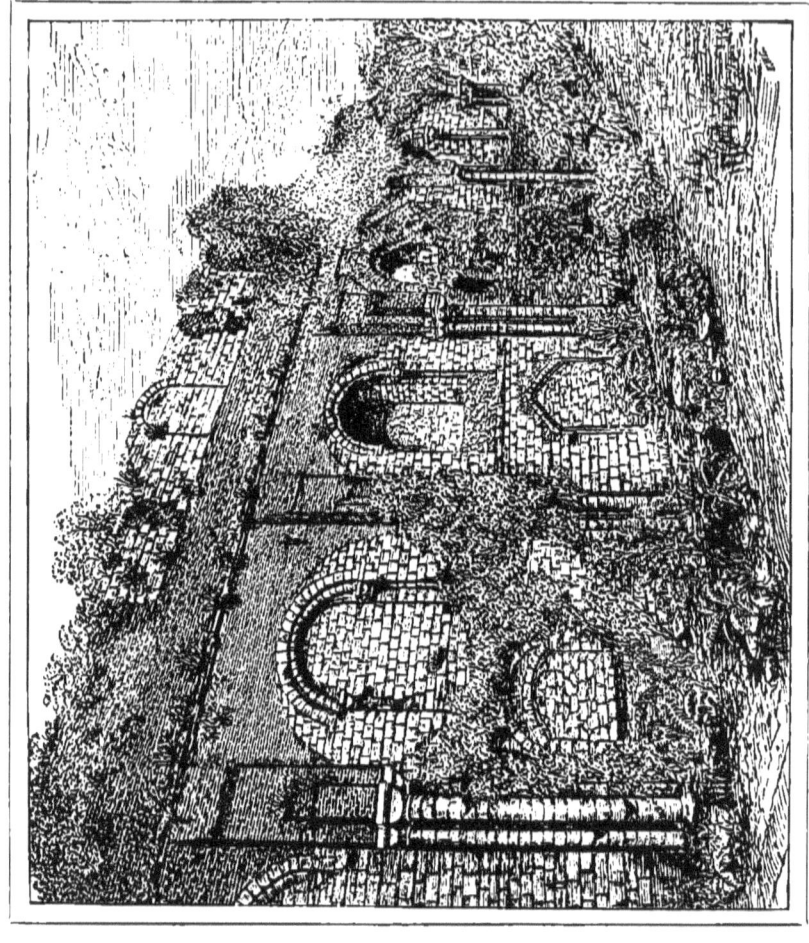

RUINS OF THE ABBEY CHURCH OF ST. AUGUSTINE.

afterwards, but became the chief defenders of the same." So runs the monk's tale, but it is to be feared that the balance of probability is in favour of Elmar's treachery. It is not likely that the men who sacked the city, and murdered Archbishop Elphege would be awed into sparing the monastery. Half a century later a new and more lasting invasion brought great changes to St. Augustine's, as well as to most of the ecclesiastical buildings in the country. The Normans destroyed to build anew, and when, in the time of Lanfranc, Scotland, the Norman, was made Abbot, he pulled down the rude Saxon church, and began to build the Norman Church of which a few columns and arches still remain. He died in 1087 and left the work to be completed by his successor Wido. When all was finished, the bones of Augustine were once more moved, to be deposited in the new Abbey, his stone coffin being secretly built into the wall of the east end of the church. About seventy years afterwards (1168) a fire broke out in the monastery, which destroyed many of the ancient records and did much damage in the church. This happened in a time of trouble and humiliation for the monastery, into which an Abbot had been intruded whom the Chapter refused to own. The monks would not let him minister in the church, or have any part in the doings of the Chapter; but he held his office, notwithstanding, during thirteen years, when he was deposed by a mandate from the Pope. We do not know to what extent the fire of 1168 rendered rebuilding necessary. In 1271 the monastery was likely to be destroyed by flood. A terrible storm arose in that year, during which there were—"thunders and lightnings and such an inundation of rain that the city of Canterbury was almost drowned. The flood was so high both in the court of the monastery and the church that they had been quite overwhelmed with water, unless the virtue of the Saints who rested there had withstood the waters. During this storm rain poured down for days as though a second universal flood was coming upon the earth; flocks and herds were swept away, and trees overturned; the flood was followed first by famine and afterwards by plague."

When the murder of Becket drew the interest and devotion of the Christian world to the shrine in Christ Church, the monks of St.

Augustine's were in danger of being neglected and forgotten. The rival Chapter spared no means to turn the whole tide of popular favour and munificence into their own channel. There was no love lost between the two communities; from the two Abbots to their lowest serving men, jealousy, hatred and malice seem to have been cherished by one against the other.

There were times when the Chapter of St. Augustine's found it hard to supply the daily wants of their large community. In the Paston Letters is one from a monk, who, writing in 1464, declares that the community were in great debt and misery, and had hardly bread to eat. There were worse times ahead, however, and the final crash came when John Essex, the seventieth Abbot, and thirty of his monks, signed the deed of dissolution, in the thirtieth year of the reign of Henry VIII. That Royal appropriator converted the monastery and its lands into a palace and deer park. His daughter Mary gave it to Cardinal Pole for his life, and her sister Elizabeth granted it to Henry, Lord Cobham, who being attainted, it reverted to the Crown. The Queen then gave it to Viscount Cranbourne, Earl of Salisbury, and subsequently it fell into the possession of Edward, Lord Wotton, of Marley. Through his family it passed to Sir Edward Hales, who married a Wotton, and ultimately to his descendant, Sir Edward Hales, of St. Stephen's.

We have touched but lightly on the chronicles, more or less historical, of the Monastery. On the history written in stone we can rely, but how much of history in books is better than fable? Somner republished copies of old Latin charters which purported to be those by which Ethelbert gave to Augustine his palace at Canterbury. But the cold blast of criticism has cast its blight on these, as on so many other interesting things in which we would fain believe. After all, these same charters, if spurious, may yet be to some extent based on originals. If forgeries they are ancient ones, and interesting. They are dated A.D. 605, in the early summer of which year Augustine is supposed to have died (there is some doubt as to the date of his death). The first charter states that King Ethelbert gives, in honour of St. Peter, land on the east side of Canterbury "that a monastery may be there erected." The second says that the King gives to God a portion of land "where he had founded a monastery." The third charter names the monk Peter, as first Abbot of the monastery, and gives to it "Chistelet otherwise called Sturiag." It also gives to the monastery a golden sceptre, and a bridle and saddle adorned with gold and precious stones. Mention is made in it of Augustine having enriched the monastery with relics of Apostles and Saints, and "other ecclesiastical ornaments," sent him from Rome. A fourth charter appoints the monastery the sole place for the burial of Kings, Archbishops and Princes. The differing degrees of assent attached to the signatures to the charter are curious, and worth briefly noting. The king "confirms" by his own hand with the sign of the Cross. Augustine "subscribed willingly." Eadbald the king's son, who afterwards became an apostate, declared himself "favourable to it." One of the king's nobles "praised it," another "consented to it," a third "approved it," and a fourth "blessed it."

Ethelbert's successor, Eadbald, built a church for the monastery, dedicated to St. Mary. He also gave "30 plough lands" in the Manor of Northbourne to it. Other royal benefactors added additional plough lands to the estates. Canute the Dane not only gave the property of the Abbey of St. Mildred, at Minster (Thanet), but presented the monks with the body of the saint, and Edward the Confessor gave "all the land he had in Fordwich."

During the greater part of the middle ages the Abbey was the most famous in England, if not in Europe, but it was not without its vicissitudes, even in the days of its glory. It had lean years as well as fat, for one of its chronicles piteously tells of food being scarce, and the cellarer so straightened, that the monks had to send to public houses for their daily quantum of ale. The Abbots were more apt in luxury perhaps than in management of the monastic exchequer, and their rivalry with Christ Church led to a costly though splendid hospitality.

CHAPTER V.

The Monastery of St. Augustine.

(Continued).

THE grand gate of St. Augustine's, at the north-west corner of the monastery, faces a small square, known since the days of Charles II. as Lady Wootton's Green. Everyone who has a sense of beauty must rejoice that this matchless gate was spared by the spoilers who destroyed the noble buildings to which it gave access. It is flanked by two octagonal towers, which rise, elegant as Saracenic minarets, above the main building, and from tower to tower springs a pointed arch with deep cut mouldings; above this is the Gate Chamber, whose mullioned windows and canopied niches form brilliant bays of an arcade of singular beauty, spanning the whole façade, and encompassing the towers on either side. The decorated battlement rises above a band of trefoiled triangles than which Gothic art never devised a more perfectly harmonious ornament.

Window of the Abbot's Chamber, St. Augustine's.

Within the front arch is a flatter one which frames in the massive doors of panelled oak. One might fancy these two arches were designed to symbolize the ideal and the actual of monastic life—the first soaring heavenward, the other drawn earthward ; the one pure as the motive, the other debased as the conduct. With such reflections we step within the gates and pass under the finely vaulted archway into the Great Court. How quiet, calm, and beautiful is the whole scene ; the green sward framed in on the one side by the buildings of the "living present," and on the other by the ruins of the past, whose crumbling remains are shadowed beneath stately trees ; here the rich line of traceried cloister, and the simple dormitories of the students ; there the noble Library with its treasures of learning, and below it the interesting crypt in which the Augustinians acquire skill in hand-labour and learn the mysteries of carpentry and building. On the other side the eye ranges from the Guest Hall and the beautiful little chapel to the distant ruins of the Abbey church over which so many changes have passed.

Few are able to realize what must have been the proportions and grandeur of that noble Abbey. The hand of time has been less ruthless than that of man ; the same spirit of barbarism which permitted a spot sacred in English history to be turned into a tavern, battered down the Abbey walls, and scattered the memorials of saints and kings. How little, alas, is left to aid us, in imagination, restore to these ruined walls their original beauty, and people these courts again !

Yet, thanks to the princely munificence of Mr. Beresford-Hope, who has built for himself an enduring monument within this ancient monastery, this first home of missionaries to the heathen English, has become a home and school for English missionaries to the heathen world. Once more peace and order reign within these precincts, and the new spirit which pervades them, links us with the memorable times of old. We think of those who have gone forth, year after year, from St. Augustine's into all the settlements of Englishmen in the " Greater Britain," into Africa, India, and the farther East ; into the Western Canadian wilds, the Australasian colonies, the West Indies, and the distant Pacific isles ; and knowing that they have proved themselves valiant soldiers of the Cross, we are reminded of the beautiful lines written by Dr. Neale, on the completion of the first solemn service of consecration in the newly founded College:—

> I see the white-wing'd vessels, that bound to realms afar,
> Go conquering and to conquer, upon their holy war ;
> No loud-voiced cannon bear they, those messengers divine
> Of England's merchant-princes, and England's battle line ;
> Yet they breast the broad Atlantic, the Polar zone they brave,
> They dash the spray-drops from their bow in that Antarctic wave ;
> The fiend that haunt's the Lion's Bay, the dagger of Japan,
> The thousand wrecks they laugh to scorn of stormy Magellan.
> Where earthly arms were weakness, and earthly gold were dross,
> Safe go they, for they carry the unconquerable Cross :
> The Cross that, planted here at first, now planted here again,
> Shall bloom and flourish in the sight of angels and of men ;
> Another St. Augustine this holy house shall grace,
> Another English Boniface shall run the Martyr's race,
> Another brave Paulinus for heathen souls shall yearn,
> Another Saint Columba rise ; another Kentigern !
> Awake, and give the blind their sight ; teach praises to the dumb,
> O Mother Church ! arise and shine, for lo ! thy light is come !
> Till all the faithful through the world, God's one elected host,
> Shall welcome the outpouring of a brighter Pentecost :
> And there shall be, and thou shalt see, throughout this earthly ball,
> One Church, one Faith, one Baptism, one God and Lord of all !

It is not possible in our days to adequately appreciate the grandeur of St. Augustine's when the all but sovereign Abbot ruled its little world ; but, aided by a fragment here and there, we may form some idea of the ancient buildings of the monastery, which extended over sixteen acres of land, and were alike magnificent in size and style. The Abbey church rose high above the surrounding edifices, as Christ Church now does over the city. Its magnificent tower, named after Ethelbert, was massive as a castle keep; its lofty walls were pierced with arcades of round arches, some of which, intersecting, formed the pointed arch which ushered in the aspiring Gothic. There were countless pillars cunningly carved in twist and spiral, with their capitals chiselled into

THE MONASTERY OF ST. AUGUSTINE.

quaint devices. This grand square tower rising to a height of 125 feet, stood at the north west corner of the Abbey church. The nave was 34 feet wide, flanked by aisles, each 19 feet wide, with lofty columns supporting the vaulted roof. Beyond were the choir and chancel with the magnificent east window (resembling, it is said, the great window of Tintern) forming a glorious background to the High Altar, within which the bones of Augustine were laid. Around were numerous other altars, all more or less resplendent in gold and jewels, and bearing saintly relics.

On the south side of the church was the porch of St. Martin, wherein Bertha was first buried; on the north side, the porch of St. Mildred. Next to the church on the north side, was the Abbot's chamber, and the Abbot's chapel, having access on one side to the church, and on the other to the Cloisters, which ran north and then east, around the Monk's garden. Beyond the Cloisters stood the Refectory, and beyond that a lordly kitchen, a splendid hexagonal building with eight columns, and, doubtless, vaulted roof. A subterranean way ran from the Kitchen to the Refectory. But yet farther to the north was the Infirmary, another massive and extensive building, with its own chapel adjoining. Then there were the Abbot's apartments, the Dormitories for the monks, and the Dungeon, with its thick walls, unpierced by door, and lighted only by a narrow window, too high to be reached by the prisoner, who was probably lowered into the place from above. Into this "Little Ease," there may have been put not merely refractory monks, but quite possibly defaulting tenants, over whom the Lord Abbot had jurisdiction. There were chambers also for royal and noble visitors, a Guest Chapel, and Guest Hall. The monastery had its own water course from the hills beyond; its noble gardens and orchards; its mortuary chapel, where the dead awaited burial; and its cemetery where, age after age, the monks of St. Augustine, and many of the citizens from without, were laid at rest.

What remains of all this? A mere fragment of Ethelbert's tower; the wall of the north aisle of the church; here and there the base of a column, or the shaft of a fallen arch; and the whole foundations of the Church buried under a mass of earth and debris, which fills up the site of the nave, and extends far into the field beyond, where a great mound marks the eastern limit, and covers the remains of the chancel. Of the other buildings of the monastery, the Guesten Hall, the foundations of the Refectory, and the Gate House, are parts of the ancient structure.

Some portion of Ethelbert's tower was still standing in the early part of this century. The achievements of the local Vandals appear to have culminated in the year 1822, when one of the most interesting and instructive fragments of early Norman work was cast to the ground. The very stones might have found tongues to swell the chorus of "shame" which rose from those who watched the stupid work of spoliation carried on. The pictures of the Tower taken about this time show a lofty pile which reared itself in massive grandeur, with here and there a remaining arch and column. It was against this beautiful ruin that local barbarians kept jamming a battering ram for days, because someone was nervous lest the solid mass which had stood for centuries should suddenly fall.

CHAPTER VI.

The Monastery of St. Augustine.

(Continued).

Door of North West Porch of the Abbey.

A VAULTED archway led from the Tower into a Galilee Porch at the west end of the church, beyond which another porch, or tower, stood at the opposite south west corner. In the recent excavations of the earth covering the site of the nave and north aisle, the bases of some of the columns of the church have been laid bare, and much of the tile flooring of the mediæval church is still *in situ*. Some of the tiles were very fine, both as to design and colour, many having the *fleur-de-lys*, others the rose, and some a circular pattern requiring four tiles to complete it. The ground sounds hollow in several places, and further digging would probably lead to some interesting discoveries.

A portion of the base of Ethelbert's Tower, still standing, enables us to judge how vast was the material it contained. The pictures of it, which can be seen in the College Library, give us a fair idea of its style. It was square in form, and the parts of two sides which now remain above the foundations indicate roughly the dimensions, its walls for some height above the ground being from ten to twelve feet thick. The columns still standing in the angles of the Tower show capitals of the earliest Norman style. The entrance into the Church through the massive wall remaining is of course the work of a later period (15th century probably), and a wonderful piece of masonry it is. The ashlar blocks of Caen stone, with which the coarse material of the tower is here arched and faced are almost absolutely perfect in surface and joint, after several hundred years of exposure.

The wall of the north aisle of the Norman church still stands, and bears above it a lofty course of brickwork of the Tudor period, added when the ruined wall of the Abbey was utilised for the new palace buildings, erected after the dissolution of the Monastery. The church to which this aisle wall belonged was the work of the two first Norman Abbots, and must have been finished just before the end of the 11th century. There are still remaining six of the original bays of the north aisle. They are separated by columns about twenty feet high, with plain Norman capitals. The Norman windows have been filled up, but the semi-circular arches are still nearly perfect. In the second bay of the aisle wall is a very early Norman arch. In the next is a pointed arch inserted, probably, at the date of the Tudor alterations. It is remarkable how admirably the stone surface of the early columns and arches has been preserved. At the extremity of the nave aisle, there is a fragment of an aisle arch ; of the choir and chancel, only the site remains ; but as the bases of the pillars and the foundations of the walls are still in the ground, we hope that the whole of them will one day be laid open.

Passing to the exterior of the north aisle wall, we are upon the site of the palace buildings of Henry VIII. ; which, earlier still, in the days of the Abbey's prosperity, was the site of the Abbot's Chamber. Still more recently, in the days of its degradation, it was turned into a fives-court and a skittle-ground for the public-house—to such base uses had the Church of St. Augustine been brought. On the east side of the court is an old wall in which a blocked-up arch marks the entrance to the Abbot's Chamber. On the other side of the wall, the bases of the numerous clustered columns on either side of the door are still to be seen; it must have been a doorway of great beauty. Over this arch was a very fine pointed window, shown in the old drawings. It suddenly fell in about forty years ago. (See initial to Chap. V.) This old wall contains a grilled opening, which formerly looked upon the Cloisters from the Abbot's larder, a spot which doubtless had a powerful attraction for the monks without. The cellarer's room was close by. There was, not long since, in this wall a rude arch of rough stones, roughly set together, probably pre-Norman. It has of late fallen in. Beyond, we have a pointed doorway, which originally opened into the Cloisters. (See initial to Chap. IV.) The north wall of the Cloisters shows traces of the sedilia for the monks. This wall contains a good deal of a curious conglomerate of shingle, naturally cemented by lime deposited by a calcareous stream. The Cloisters surrounded the monks' garden, over the walls of which we can now look into the fields beyond, but it must be remembered that the monks were wholly shut off by high walls from any chance of an outlook upon the external world.

The large field between St. Augustine's and St. Pancras, and the orchard beyond it, were formerly part of the Monastery. The whole site to the farthest boundary wall is full of roughly-rectangular mounds, marking the position of the foundations and walls which lie below. There are acres of walled chambers buried here, with doubtless many a hidden treasure amongst the *débris*. Stone and leaden coffins have been dug up here at various times; many Roman coins have been found, and other articles of great interest to the archæologist. We have seen fragments of jasper columns and marble capitals of great beauty, which were dug from one of the many chambers which are below the surface of this large meadow. Roman tiles are to be found in every part in greater abundance than the little Roman church of St. Pancras will account for.

During hot and dry weather, the position and dimensions of the

RUINS OF ETHELBERT'S TOWER; AND NORTH WEST PORCH.

buried walls are made clear by the parched and withered vegetation above them. The rectangular spaces are mostly from 18ft. to 24ft. square, and without much difficulty a ground plan of the whole could be made out. On the south side of the field is a much larger rectangular space, surrounded by walls and *débris*. This is about 80ft. wide and 100ft. in length, measured from the wall of the College. It marks the site of the east end of the Abbey-Church.

On the east front of the Refectory, there was a subterranean passage some thirty yards long at least, and about ten feet deep from the arched roof to the floor. This was probably an underground communication from the refectory to the kitchen. The foundations of the latter building remaining, indicate a grandeur in keeping with the Abbey. The size of it can be readily made out, as the pathways in the garden are laid down on its massive walls. It was hexagonal in shape, and must have been extremely spacious. A base of one of the columns which is now exposed, shows that it was grand in style as well as in size. Under the kitchen ran the water-course, supplied from the springs on Scotland Hills. Beyond the kitchen, and now beyond the boundary of the College, stand portions of the walls of the Infirmary, and, at the spot called Mount Pleasant, a part of the Infirmary Chapel. The thickness of the walls of this Chapel and Infirmary, which were but adjuncts of the Abbey, remind us how utterly different were the conditions under which mediæval builders did their work.

On the foundation of the old Refectory the College Library has been erected, a very fine hall, lofty and well lighted, with its literary treasures admirably arranged. Here also are preserved many objects of interest which the visitor should not fail to see. It is worth noticing that the fourth window on the west side frames in a view which contains no building of later date than the era of the Reformation. The view comprises the gate-house of Abbot Fyndon and the ancient buildings adjoining, while Bell Harry Tower rises majestically in the distance. The library contains several old drawings and prints of great interest as showing the actual condition of the monastery during the last two centuries. A curious relic of the public-house period is preserved in the shape of a placard which announces the opening of the gardens by "Mr. Stanmore, late of Canterbury Theatre, every Tuesday and Thursday, upon the principle of the Royal Gardens, Vauxhall; with dancing, walking the tight rope, fireworks, &c., &c."

The Refectory with its interesting crypt has been restored as nearly like the original as the few remains rendered possible. The vaulted roof of the crypt is supported on ten elegant columns, and the place is well lighted and spacious. It is put to a very practical use, being furnished with benches, lathes, and all the apparatus of the carpenter's art, for here the students are trained in such technical work as is likely to be of good service to them in their future mission-homes. For instance, one who first learned to handle the saw and the plane under this vault, has built two churches for his Dyak people in Borneo (Mr. Croysland), and numerous other illustrations might be given of the value of the instruction the students obtain from their master in carpentry. The walls of the old crypt were lined with painted panelling, a portion of which was many years ago carried away to be used, we believe, at the George and Dragon Inn.

CHAPTER VII.

The Monastery of St. Augustine.

(Continued).

Bay of Tudor Wall in the Warden's garden.

N the beautiful chequered wall of the Warden's garden there is an interesting relic of the Tudor period, when the Abbey was converted into a palace for Henry VIII. The chequered squares of stone and flints are singularly effective, and the proportions of the recesses by which the wall is divided into bays very harmonious. A single bay is sketched in the initial to this chapter.

On the west side of the Great Court are the Guest Hall and Chapel, access to both being gained by an old stone staircase, part of the original building. The hall is a very fine apartment, a restoration of the ancient Guest Hall, erected by Abbot Fyndon at the close of the 13th century. Its splendid oak roof is in part ancient; the windows are reproductions of the old ones, as nearly as could be ascertained from fragments of tracery found in the ruins. Much as it is now it must have been when royal and lordly guests were entertained within its walls, and when Queen Bess, seated on the dais, in all her glory of paint and jewels, received the homage and flattery of her great courtiers. Charles 1st and Charles 2nd, were also entertained under the same roof. The former ill-fated sovereign lodged in the Abbey on the occasion of his marriage; the latter on his journey to London at the Restoration. At the marriage of Charles 1st Orlando Gibbons of the Chapel Royal came down to officiate as organist, caught the small pox, and died here. He was buried in the Cathedral. If the old walls could but repeat to us the conversations to which they resounded on some of these historic occasions! But after all, the grand old room is put to better use than the casual entertainment of Tudors or Stuarts. It is now the Common hall of the Missionary College. Here the students take their meals in company with the Warden, the Sub-Warden, and Fellows, who sit at the upper table on the dais. The Warden's chair is an elaborate, carved oak piece, probably old Flemish. It was presented to the College by the munificent founder. On the wall behind hangs a fine mosaic, a copy by Salviati, of a celebrated Mosaic in St. Mark's Venice. It represents the Saviour, seated on the throne of judgment, with the great book open in his hands. Near the dais is an old painting of considerable interest, which was once, we believe, the fire-place ornament of a neighbouring tavern. It represents St. Augustine's, probably at some time during the last century, and shows Ethelbert's Tower and other buildings of the monastery now no longer standing. On the walls of the hall are excellent portraits of the following benefactors of the College—Bishop Coleridge, who was chaplain to Archbishop Howley at the same time as Mr. Lyall (afterwards Dean of Canterbury). The two chaplains were so much alike in features that they were constantly mistaken for each other—The Rev. Edward Coleridge, who gave the first impulse to the movement for founding a missionary college, and wrote many thousands of letters to gather in funds for its permanent endowment—Dr. Lochée, who gave his gratuitous and valuable services to the College for 25 years, as lecturer on medicine—Canon Gilbert, who was one of the choir boys of Canterbury, and was advanced from the Choristers' School to the King's School. There he so well applied himself to study that he gained a scholarship at Cambridge; he received the living of Grantham, and was made honorary Canon of Lincoln. By his will be founded three scholarships for students in that diocese. He made many benefactions to charities during his life, and bequeathed his plate and books to the College of St. Augustine.

From the Hall we pass to the Chapel. This is built on the site of the old Guest's Chapel, but only a portion of the walls and the beautiful west windows are ancient. All the windows of the Chapel contain fine painted glass, of excellent design and colour, by Willement. A pierced oak screen of good execution and style, separates the ante-chapel from the nave. The latter is admirably fitted with carved oak stalls for the Warden, Fellows and students, the stalls being copies of ancient miserere seats. The whole Chapel is very beautiful. The east window, of five lights, contains St. Gregory, St. Augustine, the Baptism of John, the Adoration, and the First Miracle. A south window, of four lights, contains the prophets Isaiah, Jeremiah, Ezekiel and Daniel. The north window contains the Four Evangelists. The Reredos of marble, and the mosaic panels (the gift of Canon Bailey) admirably harmonize. The floor tiles are equally beautiful in design and colour, and are copies of original tiles of the 13th or 14th century.

Below the Chapel is an extended reproduction of the ancient crypt, which was probably used by the monks as a mortuary chapel for the Abbey. It is divided into two portions—the eastern is now used as a little Guild-chapel by the students. It contains a small bronze figure of the Good Shepherd, the pedestal on which it stands having a representation of the expulsion of our first parents from Eden. A tablet commemorates the first Warden of the College—Bishop Coleridge (of Barbadoes), who died in 1849. In the other portion of the crypt a number of mural panels bear brief memorials of students of St. Augustine's, who have already passed to their rest. Many of these terse records of young lives are full of touching interest, as they show how wide is the field over which the missionary seed of the College is scattered. Here we are reminded of poor Kallihirua, the Eskimo convert and student, who was baptised at St. Martin's, Capt. Ommaney, who brought him to this country, acting as sponsor. The tablet to the memory of this Christian child of the North, in whom so much interest was taken during his life in England, runs thus:—

"ERASMUS AUGUSTINE KALLIHIRUA,
Arrived from 76° N.L., Nov. 1851,
Baptised Advent Sunday, 1853,
Deceased June 14, 1856,
Newfoundland."

Other memorials perpetuate the memory of Kona, who came hither from Caffraria in 1861, and who fell an early victim to disease at Grahamstown in 1865; Moshueshua, who left Basuto land in 1861, and died at Hereford in two short years; and of Mahmoud Effendi, who was expelled from Turkey on having married a Christian English lady. The same wall which bears these interesting records of departed students, has two sculptured groups in high-relief. One which represents Gregory in the market-place of Rome, speaking with the fair young English slaves, has been erected in memory of the Rev. H. J. Hutchesson. The other represents Augustine preaching to Ethelbert. This is interesting in itself as a work of art, and also as the result of self denial. It was erected by the students in memory of their deceased companions, and they collected the cost of the group by abstaining from the use of sugar for a considerable time.

On leaving the Chapel, visitors who are interested in the perfection of the builder's art should notice two remarkable buttresses of the building. They are composed of small flints beautifully shaped into squares. Squared flints are not uncommon in Kent, but we have never seen any to equal these. The edges of each flint are perfectly rectangular, and the exterior surface is smooth and flat. They must have been fashioned by Abbot Fyndon's skilful artificers, for the buttresses originally belonged to the Gate House.

Below the Guest Hall is the present kitchen of the College. It is a part of the original structure of the hall, as the old oak beams remaining are sufficient to show. This was the kitchen of that outer circle of the Abbey in which the Abbot's guests and retainers were lodged, and,

THE MONASTERY OF ST. AUGUSTINE.

no doubt, munificently entertained. The grand kitchen we have previously mentioned was situated within the inner circle which was closely sealed to the general world. Here, no doubt, some of those sumptuous feasts were prepared, which the old records tell us were so often served at Canterbury, on the occasions of Royal visits. The kitchen was in the first part of the present century the bar of the public house. Between this and the Manciple's Room, at the gate, is the chamber which we have spoken of as the prison. Until recently it had no doorway. If it was really used as a dungeon, in the olden times, the prisoner must have been lowered into it from the ancient looking chamber above. It was not a "black hole," however, for light would have been admitted by the small loop in the thick wall.

We have now made the entire round of the ancient buildings of the Abbey, and have returned to the Gate House at which we entered. Passing into the lodge, we ascend a staircase into the fine old room over the arch of the gate. This was the chamber in which Queen Elizabeth slept when holding her Court at Canterbury, and it was occupied by Charles I. when he received at St. Augustine's his French bride, Henrietta Maria. The room is now used as a museum for the Missionary College. It contains many objects of interest sent home by the students from their distant mission homes. During the period of the desecration, when the wall of the Abbey church served for a tennis court, this royal chamber was used as a malt-house and sometimes as a cock-pit.

Before quitting the spot in which we have spent many pleasant hours, we ascend, by a spiral stone staircase, to the roof of the Gate-house and obtain a bird's-eye view of the whole extent of the monastery. What a panorama of English history lies before us! There is scarcely an age or epoch in the roll of nineteen centuries but has its record here. The long line of unbroken roof to the left covers the rooms of the present Collegians,—no monkish cells, but pleasant little chambers into which the young missionaries may retire for meditation and study by day, fired, let us hope, by a nobler faith, and loftier ambition than was ever developed in those old ruined cloisters in the distance. Thus as we look on the training-home of the missionaries of our own day, so may we cast our glance beyond, to the site of the little Christian church of Roman times, over which the flood of Saxon barbarism swept, but happily did not endure. There is the pathway Bertha trod as she went out to pray at St. Martin's. There is the spot where the gentle Queen was laid to rest. There the burial place of Augustine and his immediate successors; of Ethelbert and the Christian kings of Kent. The ruined Abbey stands on the site of one which pagan Danes destroyed. It was itself the handwork of two races and of several eras—of Norman and of Early English builders—while it bears in its Tudor masonry the record of the dissolution of the Abbey, and the incoming of a new order, and a reformed Faith. Thus Roman, Briton, Saxon, Dane, Norman, and Englishman have all left their traces within the boundaries of St. Augustine's.

CHAPTER VIII.

The Hospital of St. John.

Old stone Font
St. John's Hospital.

N or about the year 1084, Archbishop Lanfranc founded at Canterbury two hospitals or almshouses. One of these is in Northgate Street, and is dedicated to Saint John ; the other at Harbledown, is dedicated to Saint Nicholas. The first was designed for the support of maimed, sick, and weak persons of both sexes. The other was a lazar-house for lepers, and was placed, like all similar institutions in the middle ages, by the side of the highway, at a little distance outside the town.

We first visit the Hospital of St. John. In the middle of busy Northgate there stands an interesting old house, timber-panelled and gable-roofed, over a fine wooden arch. We pass through this from the noisy street, and enter a quiet enclosure, a peaceful haven of repose. The green sward is framed in by grey rambling lines of buildings ; some, the ruined remains of long past ages ; others, the present homes of those who are themselves quietly dropping into decay. On the right is the old church, where the brothers and

THE GATE OF ST. JOHN'S HOSPITAL.

sisters, who are still able to get out, meet and worship, and beyond it the churchyard where former generations of brothers and sisters of St. John's have been laid to rest. We wander among the graves, and see by the inscriptions on the headstones that this retreat from the cares and worries of the struggling world must ensure ripe old age. Presently we find that one of the sisters of the hospital has just passed her ninetieth birthday.

Around the churchyard are some interesting ruins, which would be much improved by clearing away the old sheds and outhouses erected against them. These walls are massive portions of what was probably the original buildings of Lanfranc. His disciple and biographer, Eadmer, dignifies them with the name of palace. It is evident by the external appearance of the chapel, that it was originally much larger in size. Gostling makes complaint of the unnecessary demolition of the ancient buildings, perpetrated about the middle of the last century— "the bells having been sold, the steeple and north aisle taken down, as were many of the old houses, and smaller and less convenient ones erected in their room ; a stone wall was also taken away, which sheltered the whole from the cold north-west wind blowing over the river and meadow land, and, being pentised over-head, was called by the poor people their cloisters, under which they used to walk or sit, and converse with each other on the benches." Gostling adds satirically, "all this was done *by way of improvement* about thirty years ago." (1747). We can imagine with what indignant emphasis the genial and gossipping old minor canon would have shaken his walking stick (which is now suspended over his portrait in the City Museum) at such barbarism. The old wall on the north-west side of the Chapel still contains some interesting remains of the early Norman masonry, with round-headed doors, and windows, having only slight and coarsely-cut moulding. Within the Church, the west doorway of which is early Norman, the chief object of interest remaining is the ancient font of stone, roughly circular in shape, without ornament, and with two curiously-shaped handles. The east window was still in the last century filled with painted glass, containing figures of the twelve Apostles, but this has entirely disappeared, as have also the pulpit and some other woodwork, said to have been good examples of Tudor carving.

The "City Fathers" of the Tudor age had themselves some depredations to answer for, as in 1507 a complaint was made to the Archdeacon that the Mayor of Canterbury had carried off the ornaments of the Chapel, such as a chalice, a paten of silver, a surplice, and a bell.

In the south-west corner of the enclosure is the old hall and kitchen, believed to date from the 16th century. The hall, which is over the kitchen, is entered by a narrow staircase. It still contains the old central dining-table and benches, of rough-hewn oak, much more massive than convenient, the space between the fixed seat and the table being evidently designed to accommodate brethren of portly form and aldermanic dimensions. Here, no doubt, for many ages the inmates of the hospital have had their annual feast, as they do now, on St. John's Day. One of the old registers gives the cost of the Midsummer feast in 1638, when a sum of £3 6s. 10d. was expended. Some of the items are curious and interesting. The bill of fare comprised 80lbs. of beef, at 3d. per lb. A calf cost 18s. Two lambs cost the same amount. Three "coople" of chicken cost half-a-crown. To wash down these solid comforts, the brethren and sisters appear to have required "halfe a barrel of beere," costing 3s. 2d., a gallon of "sacke," 3s. 4d., a "pottle of claritt and a pottle of white wine," in all 2s. 8d. "Beere to make the serving men drinke that brought meat to our feast," cost 2d. "Beere for the kitchen" cost 4d., and the "cooke for drissing the dinner" was paid handsomely,—4s. The "woman that helped in the kitchen" got 6d., and the "two turnspets," 8d. The "spets" they turned are still to be seen in the kitchen below. They are 8 or 10 feet long, and would have served to roast a royal joint. There is a curious old fork, also of which the "cooke" of 1638 might have made use.

The hall contains two fine old oak chests, in which are some things of antiquarian interest. There is a large sword, having no doubt a history, but about which we could get no information. An old pewter drinking flagon, from which doubtless the brethren had, many time and oft, quaffed a refreshing draught, bears a coat of arms, and the following inscription :—" The gift of Robart Mascoll, Esq., to St. John's Hospitall, the 24th day of June, 1659." There are several old pewter dishes also, and three ancient wooden bowls with medallions ; one having the Tudor rose, another the Virgin and Child, another the sacred monogram, I.H.S. Besides these there are a very curious alms box, in shape much like a Roman lamp, an old folio copy of Fox's Book of Martyrs, and other articles of interest.

Lanfranc endowed St. John's Hospital and that of Harbledown with £70 per annum, out of the manor of Reculver and Boughton-under-Blean. His next successor increased the endowment to £80 for each hospital. This would have been an ample income according to the value of money at that time, and indeed the number of the brothers and sisters appears to have been originally much larger and to have gradually decreased. Thus in the latter part of the 14th century the hospital had one hundred inmates, a century later eighty only, and when another century had passed the number provided for, in Archbishop Parker's statutes, was sixty (including out-brothers and sisters).

Anciently, a few weeks before and after the two festivals of St. John and Christmas, the brethren sent out certain of their number to travel up and down the country begging for alms. They bore with them a latin letter of authorization, bearing the seal of the hospital. This letter, after recounting the indulgences granted by the Archbishops to benefactors of St. John's, made abundant promises of future rewards for present charitable gifts of gold or silver.

It declared that there were in the hospital one hundred brothers and sisters who, between them, daily said no fewer than thirty thousand Paternosters and Ave Marias, the benefits of which, with innumerable prayers, fasts, and penances, would be shared by all their benefactors. (This curious letter is given in full by Duncombe.) The custom of sending out begging brothers and sisters was certainly kept up as late as 1585. Archbishop Parker in 1560 drew up statutes for the government of the Hospital, and these are supposed to have remained in force until our own time. Some of the orders and rules have ceased to be observed. For instance, the brethren and sisters were "to diligently come to the church twice in the day to offer up their common prayers unto Almighty God, and attentively to hear God's Holy Scripture read." If any absented themselves without permission, or being present, "jangled," or slept during prayers, then "if after two admonitions given by the prior to amend that fault, the party eftsoones commit the like offense that brother or sister, whither it be, shall be punished in the stocks one half day or more." If the offender still proved refractory there was the penalty of expulsion to be looked forward to. For more heinous offences, such as drunkenness, brawling, or blasphemous swearing, the punishment on the first occasion was to sit in the stocks one day and a night, with bread and water, the second time two days and two nights, the third time three days and three nights; if after that the offence was repeated the sinner was "to be expulsed and driven out of the house for ever."

The ancient charters and records of St. John's and St. Nicholas' Hospitals were carefully set in order and many of them transcribed by the Rev. Henry Hall, M.A., who was appointed Librarian at Lambeth by Archbishop Potter (1744), and subsequently became Rector of St. Michael's, Harbledown. His work was completed by the Rev. Dr. Beauvoir, whose MSS. "Liber Hospitalium Archiepiscopi" is at Lambeth. Duncombe, the historian of the Hospitals, has quoted largely from these records, which contain many things of interest to the antiquarian and historian.

It is pleasant to see the care taken by the inmates of their plots of garden; to observe their happy and cheerful demeanour; and to know that this interesting and valuable institution is admirably administered under the Wardenship of the Bishop of Dover, as Archdeacon of Canterbury.

On the other side of Northgate Street, immediately opposite the hospital, formerly stood the gateway leading to the ancient church of St. Gregory, also a foundation of Archbishop Lanfranc, intended for secular priests, whose duty it was to administer spiritual comfort to the poor of the hospital, and to officiate at the burial of their dead. Leland states that the church was converted into a priory for Black or regular canons, in the time of Henry I. No vestige of the priory remains.

CHAPTER IX.

The Hospital of St. Nicholas, Harbledown.

Old Alms-box, St. Nicholas'.

OUT of the city, but intimately connected with it, is the old Hospital of St. Nicholas. Thither, on a lovely summer afternoon, we make our way, past old Westgate tower which, hoary as it is, lacks three out of the eight centuries to which St. Nicholas can lay claim. We strike across the fields to the foot of the hill, where the old Pilgrims' Way joins the high road. Few who enter this ancient lane think that for at least two thousand years it has been a beaten track, for it leads across the fields and hop gardens to the British camp in Bigbury Wood. It was also the end of the Pilgrims' Way, which ran across three counties, from the Hampshire port, over the Surrey downs, the woods and vales of Kent, to the city of Becket. For many an age that long thin line bore its continuous stream of life; thousands and tens of thousands of rich and poor, prince and peasant, gallant knight and doughty burgher, natives and foreigners, horsemen and pedestrians passed that way. We take our stand at the corner of the old lane, and watch in imagination the motley stream empty itself into the main road, crowded with its own incessant current of curious and pious pilgrims.

Tempting as the fancy is, however, we must not linger to indulge in day dreams, but continue our way to Harbledown. From the hill we get the finest distant view of the Cathedral. On such a summer's day as this one can most fully appreciate the exquisite beauty and the massive supremacy of the noble pile. It rises above the city like a great rock in an open plain, and as the sun lights up every niche and crevice in the towers, the giant seems clad in gems. How thankful one ought to be that in days when the souls of the builders were full of beauty, the work of their hands was made so strong and enduring.

We turn the brow of the hill and descend to the hollow in which the old village lies nestled. Its position is extremely beautiful; viewed from the fields above the hill, and behind Harbledown church, a more lovely landscape is not to be met with even in the garden of Kent.

At the foot of the hill we reach the ancient gateway of the Hospital, beside which there still stands a fine old yew. A companion tree was standing not many years since, but it has disappeared. The old gateway bears signs of great antiquity, and probably its rough and massive timbers have stood for centuries, though it is doubtful to what age it actually belongs. Formerly the roadway was deeper, and a longer flight of steps led to the entrance. At these steps the brethren used to show to travellers their far famed relics of Thomas à Becket, and solicit alms of the passers by.

But the foundation of St. Nicholas goes back to a more remote age than that which brought pilgrims to Becket's shrine. It was founded by Archbishop Lanfranc, as a Lazar House, or hospital for lepers, in or about 1084. The necessity of providing, at that early date, refuges for sufferers from leprosy shows that the dreadful disease was not, as very often stated, first introduced into this country by returning Crusaders, the first Crusade having taken place twelve years later than the foundation of the Hospital. It might have been first imported into England by returning pilgrims from the Holy Land at an earlier date; it was in any case to be found at Canterbury while the Conqueror reigned over

England, and the learned Lanfranc ruled the Church. It would be interesting to know when the last of the lepers disappeared from this hospital in the Blean, and when a new order of inmates began to be settled there, but we have no information on the point, the historical memorials of St. Nicholas being meagre in the extreme.

Doorway of St. Nicholas'.

The hospital of Harbledown was, as Somner called it, "the other twin" of St. John. It had a like endowment and similar statutes. Anciently St. Nicholas' appears to have been a rectory, but in 1342 Archbishop Stratford united it to East Bridge Hospital, obliging the latter to provide a chaplain for it. A few years later a perpetual chantry was founded, the priest of which lived at Clavering. The chantry was abolished at the Reformation. The number of inmates at Harbledown was much larger during the middle ages than it has been in modern times. Its income from the Archiepiscopal funds was supplemented by the alms of the faithful, and the brothers and sisters, like those of St. John, went out at certain times on begging expeditions. The old deeds of benefactions to the Hospital contain some curious grants. Thus, in 1379, one Wm. Yue gives an annual grant of two cercells (wild fowl), one-third of a hen, one third of half a hen, and 15 eggs.

When the tide of devotion set in towards Becket's tomb, the hospitallers of St. Nicholas must have flourished. Many a broad noble and many a mark, no doubt, dropped into the alms-box, for plenty of company passed that way, high and mighty travellers many of them. There were few probably of the pre-Reformation monarchs who did not visit Canterbury, and, as their way lay past St. Nicholas, we may feel sure that they either visited the hospital, or gave alms at the gate. Hither came Henry II. from Southampton, along the Pilgrims' Way above alluded to. He alighted and entered the Church of St. Nicholas, whence he walked barefooted to the Cathedral. "For the love of St. Thomas" Henry gave in grant twenty marks of rent to the Hospital. Here passed, twenty years later, his son Richard, who had landed at Sandwich after his release from captivity. Though he had a vast deal of work to do in a few brief weeks, Cœur-de-Lion would not have left St. Nicholas unnoticed. Whether, a little later, John, on his way to Dover, would stop to visit the Hospital is doubtful, but he was often in the neighbourhood. Edward I. and the noble Queen Eleanor passed on their return from Palestine, and tradition runs that the Black Prince, returning from his victory of Poictiers with his royal prisoner (King John of France), visited the church and Hospital. Close at hand there still remains what is known as the Black Prince's well, a spring on the hill side, behind the Hospital. A round arch has been built over it, and it is surrounded with ferns and flowers, a few steps leading down to the water. It is said that at this well the hero of Cressy and Poictiers drank as he returned home to die. A little later his remains were carried by the same spot to be buried in the Cathedral.

THE HOSPITAL OF ST. NICHOLAS, HARBLEDOWN. 55

The enclosure contains the dwellings of nine brothers and seven sisters, comfortable cottages ranged on either side of a hall or frater-house. Opposite them is the venerable old church of St. Nicholas, with its great ivy tree clinging to the ancient tower. Most of the church is of later date than the building of Lanfranc; but some interesting portions of the original are preserved in the present building; these include the round arch of the west door, a pillar and capital on the north side of the nave, the circular arches of that side, and a small round headed window. There is a trace of the ancient rood-loft; here and there a few fragments of old glass remain, and there are signs of frescoes having formerly adorned the walls. In the floor are some very early tiles, and in the chancel there is an ancient tomb-recess.

The churchyard of the Hospital, from which there is a lovely view of wooded hill and valley, is studded with memorials of past brothers and sisters, the ages recorded being most frequently beyond the fourscore years.

The Hall is not of interest in itself, but contains articles of unquestionable antiquity. There is a quaint old chest, the cover of which appears to be a rough-hewn portion of an old tree trunk. In this no doubt the treasures of the Hospital were formerly preserved, but they are now kept in a more convenient place, and the Prior sets them all before the visitor, with a list of the "Relics of St. Thomas à Becket." While he produces them we read on the wall as follows :—" The ancient building of this Hospital, being utterly ruined and decayed, it was repaired A.D. 1674 in this form of a Frater House, and six houses on each side, the charge of the whole building amounting to the sum of £200, whereof £100 were given by Archbishop Sheldon and £50 by the Dean and Chapter of Canterbury. Mr. John Somner gave £50 towards the new dwellings of this Hospital." On the walls hangs the coat of arms of the present Master of the Hospital, the Bishop of Dover, as Archdeacon of Canterbury. In one of the windows is a stained glass panel containing the arms of Archbishop Abbott.

The so-called relics of St. Thomas are mostly, we fear, apocryphal, but one is possibly a genuine memento of the murdered Archbishop, and the other articles are ancient and interesting. They include a curious old alms-box with a chain attached. It was such a box as this, no doubt, which long after Lanfranc's death the leper inmates of the Hospital held out to wayfarers who passed through the Blean Forest. We can imagine how gaunt and ghastly figures would, from the old steps, proclaim their terrible misfortune, and solicit the charity of the faithful. They dared not approach travellers, but they used to put out a long pole with a box hanging from it, wherein a coin might be dropped. The old alms-box which is still preserved at St. Nicholas' is certainly centuries old, and was probably that in which the gentle Erasmus dropped his offering after inspecting the relics. He was then travelling from Canterbury to London with Dean Colet, the founder of St. Paul's School. Erasmus himself gives an account of the visit. As the two travellers approached the Hospital, on their way to London, an aged almsman came down the steps, and having sprinkled the visitors with holy water, proceeded to exhibit for their veneration that most choice and sacred relic—the upper leather of the shoe of St. Thomas. When this saintly treasure was offered them to kiss, Colet's indignation knew no bounds, nor did he hesitate to express his contempt and disgust in language more forcible than polite.

Of this incident, so significant of the disposition of the two Reformers, Stanley characteristically says:—"In the meeting of that old man with the two strangers in the lane at Harbledown, how completely do we read in miniature the whole history of the coming revolution of Europe."

Erasmus says that the shoe-leather of the Saint contained a crystal. The shoe-leather has disappeared, but the crystal which is supposed to have sparkled on the foot of Becket is possibly the same as that which is still preserved at Harbledown, fixed in the bottom of an old maple bowl. There is another maple bowl, belonging to the Hospital, which has long been an object of great interest to antiquarians. It is a good specimen of a 14th century mazer bowl, and was annually used on the feast of St. Nicholas. Let into the bottom of it is a finely executed silver-gilt medallion which bears, in basso relievo, a mounted figure of a

THE HOSPITAL OF ST. NICHOLAS, HARBLEDOWN.

knight in armour slaying a dragon, a lion lying near. The knight is the Guy of Warwick, famed in mediæval story. The inscription round the medallion has been somewhat of a puzzle to archæologists. It runs thus—GY DE WARWYC : ADANOVN : NECI OCCIS : LE DRAGOVN :

This ancient work of art is specially valuable and interesting, because it connects the obscure legend of Guy and the dragon with an episode in English history. The knight's shield bears the arms of Beauchamp, whence it is inferred that the knight is intended for Guy Beauchamp, and the dragon for the hated favourite of Edward II., Piers Gaveston, who met his fate at the hands of the remorseless earl of Warwick. There are other articles, ancient and interesting, among the relics and curiosities of Harbledown, but undoubtedly the chief attraction of St. Nicholas' lies in the associations which cluster around it, and which still draw pilgrims to the spot of which five hundred years ago Chaucer wrote these lines :—

> "Wete ye not wher stondeth a litel town
> Which that yclepèd is Bob-up-and-down
> Under the Blee in Canterbury way?"

CHAPTER X.

East Bridge Hospital.

AST Bridge Hospital, or the Hospital of St. Thomas, was founded for the accommodation of poor pilgrims, whom the renown of the murdered Becket drew to his shrine at Canterbury. The passion for pilgrimages was not confined to the nobler and wealthier orders; there were others who could neither hire horse nor pay for hostelry, and who were content to travel many a weary mile on foot along the pilgrim ways, receiving the alms of their more fortunate fellow-travellers, and lodging as best they could at the various stages on their journey. There were no workhouses or vagrant wards in those days; but there was a generally-recognised obligation to find a dole of food and a night's shelter for any poor travellers, more especially for such as might be on their way to visit some sacred spot or relics. Hospitals designed to accommodate such wayfarers were commonly founded during the middle ages. Such was the object and the use of the Hospital of St. Thomas, in the High-street.

The date of the foundation is uncertain, but it must have been as early as the beginning of the 13th century, for by a Bull of Innocent III., there was, in the year 1203, united with it the adjacent hospital founded by William Cokyn or Cockyn. There appears to have been some tradition apparently ascribing the foundation to Archbishop Becket, but this probably originated from the fact that it was used by pilgrims to Becket's shrine. As Battely puts it, if Becket had been the actual founder, "it would not have been passed over in silence by those who made it their chief work to recommend this saint to the highest esteem and veneration of all men." As no mention of his founding this hospital was made by his early eulogists, it is not likely that he was its originator. It had certainly, however, been erected within a few years of his death.

The first benefactor to the hospital, of which record remains (1200), was Archbishop Hubert Walter, who was contemporary with Richard I. and King John. He endowed it with the tithes of Westgate mill and of certain other mills. In his time lived the above-mentioned Wm. Cokyn, a worthy citizen who founded his hospital in St. Peter's-street. This he gave over to Archbishop Hubert, to be united with Eastbridge. The next Archbishop (Stephen Langton) confirmed the gift of Blean Church and parsonage, by Hamo de Crevequeur, to the Eastbridge Hospital, an appanage which it still retains.

The fame of Becket as a saint, and the admirable advertising by the monks of Christ Church of the miraculous cures wrought at his shrine, proved an irresistible attraction to the countless numbers who, in that superstitious age, sought either physical or spiritual benefit from pilgrimage or penance. They flocked in vast numbers to Canterbury, and the hospital of St. Thomas was open day and night to receive, to welcome, and to entertain poor pilgrims who could not afford to pass on to the spacious halls of the "Chequers"—Chaucer's famous hostelry.

But in the history of all human institutions, the ebb succeeds the flood; and there came a time when the hospital of St. Thomas fell into decay, for we find that no later than 1343, Archbishop Stratford (who was the next of its great benefactors) put on record the fact that this hospital, "founded for the receiving, lodging, and sustaining of poor pilgrims, was but meanly endowed, and that the buildings belonging to it were in a ruinous condition." It had by this time in fact fallen in the way of those who covet their neighbours' goods, as it is declared that "lands in Heron, Reculvre, Swalclif, Chistelet, and Beaksborn," had been alienated upon pretence of being chantry lands.

It appears that, although it had been granted charters, it had not hitherto received rules for its proper government. The Archbishop framed statutes and regulations, and established it, as he no doubt imagined, on a permanent foundation, but the history of almost all these old hospitals and charities shows that, even in the middle ages, the wills and wishes of pious founders were set aside. Its revenues arose from lands and tenements in Canterbury, Harbledown, and Birchington, as well as at Blean, the Manor of Blean and Hoath Court being settled upon it by Thomas de Roos, of Chilham. It was ordained that the master of the hospital should be in priest's orders, and should keep a vicar under him. A grant, then no doubt held to be of great importance was made to pilgrims dying within the hospital, that they should have the right of burial in the cemetery of Christ Church.

The statutes contemplated no needless loitering on the part of pilgrims, who were expressly to get but "one night's lodging and entertainment," and then to make way for other comers. There were to be twelve beds in the hospital, and an aged woman had to provide all necessaries for the pilgrims, at the cost of not more than fourpence a head.

A few years later, King Edward III. was among the benefactors to the charity, on which he bestowed the "Chaunge" in Canterbury—a Royal Exchange of unknown antiquity, the site of which was in All Saints' parish, with an entrance from the High-street.

Stratford's statutes did not preserve the hospital from spoliation. Somner tells us that "in the beginning of the reign of Elizabeth, the lands and tenements belonging to the hospital—yea, and the hospital itself, were occupied and possessed by private persons." Archbishop Parker recovered these properties, and refounded the hospital (1569) "for the reception of poor and maimed soldiers that should pace backwards and forwards through Canterbury," and for the support of a school. He restored the house, and laid down ordinances which, whilst suitable

THE HALL OF EAST BRIDGE HOSPITAL.

to the times in which he lived, were yet in unison with the intentions of the former founders.

Archbishop Parker also founded out of the funds of the hospital two "Canterbury Scholarships" at Corpus Christi College, Cambridge, each of the yearly value of £3 6s. 8d. This arrangement was to endure for 200 years, but within a single life-time ruin and robbery were again at work. A commission under Sir James Hales, appointed by Elizabeth, reported that "the hospital house stood ruinated, and that neither Master nor brethren were resident or dwelling of long time, the house let into tenements for yearly rent, the beds that were wont to lodge and harbour poor people, resorting hither, were gone, and sold contrary to the old order and foundation of the same, and the said hospital to be relinquished and concealed from her Majesty." The Queen decided that this robbery of the poor should be repaired. She carried out her decision in true Tudor fashion, by giving the property to one of her gentlemen pensioners, a certain John Farnham, who transferred it to one Hayes for £550, and the balance of a debt. Later on, however, (1584) the hospital found a friend in Archbishop Whitgift, who, after a troublesome lawsuit, actually succeeded in recovering the property which had been filched from the poor. He obtained an Act of Parliament for the more permanent establishment of the charity, and framed the statutes under which the hospital is still governed. In the same year the Dean and Chapter gave the small bell for the chapel, called the Wackeral. Later benefactors among the Archbishops were Juxon, Sheldon, and Sancroft.

It will be seen that East Bridge Hospital is of deep interest, not only from the antiquity of its buildings, but as illustrating the peculiarities of life and manners in the middle ages. It stands in the High Street, at the spot where the chief branch of the divided Stour passes under the old East bridge, or King's bridge, as it was sometimes called from the King's mill which stood next to it, opposite the Hospital.

We enter the hospital by an ancient arched doorway, whence a few steps lead into a vaulted hall, the floor of which is much below the present level of the street. A flight of steps leads to the ancient refectory, in which the pilgrims were received and entertained. The refectory is separated from the passage to the dwelling rooms of the inmates by a row of three octagonal pillars, with capitals of a transition character, supporting early-pointed arches. The columns are much out of the perpendicular, and it is evident that, owing to the nearness to the river, and the frequency with which it was formerly flooded, the foundation must have sunk at an early period. The most interesting feature of the hall at present remaining is a large fragment of an ancient wall painting; the colours are still remarkably vivid, and much of the detail can be readily distinguished, although the chief painting was probably executed in the 14th century. This valuable relic of mediæval art was discovered during some alterations carried on in 1879. The workmen, in removing the accumulation of whitewash, came upon traces of figures. Unfortunately they did not recognise the importance of their discovery, and went on scraping for some time until the prioress, happening to learn what had been found, informed the Master of the hospital. Then the work was stopped, and means taken to remove the rest of the whitewash with great care. A huge fireplace and chimney built against the wall being removed, the painting was gradually brought to view. In the centre is a fine vesica, enclosing a picture of Our Saviour enthroned. This part of the work is evidently the most ancient, and it was certainly the finest in regard to art. The emblems of the four Evangelists surround the central figure, and the whole is enclosed in a circle. Below is another painting of Christ and the Apostles at the Last Supper, Jesus handing the sop to Judas. On one side of the central design is a representation (probably of later date, and more rudely executed) of the murder of Becket. On the other side another picture, unfortunately for the most part destroyed, apparently pourtrayed Henry the Second's penance at Becket's Shrine. These treasures of early art were coated before the time of James I. with a thick layer of whitewash, for upon this barbarous covering had been painted the Royal arms, and the arms of Archbishop Abbot. The utmost care and delicacy were required on the part of the accomplished architect Mr. James Neale, F.S.A., who carried out the restoration of these interesting buildings, in order to preserve the ancient pictures. Standing in this Refectory, it requires no great stretch of imagination to people it once more with dust stained and foot-sore pilgrims gazing with reverent eyes on the picture of Christ, and probably still more devoutly on that of Becket, for in the age we speak of more reverence was paid to the Saint than to the Saviour.

From this hall we enter the chapel of the Hospital, a fine chamber lighted by three traceried windows of the 14th century. This was till recently used as a school, but has now been restored, to be used for divine worship. It contains remains of an open timber roof. At the East end is a Table of the Commandments, written in 1634, and below this an old oak reading desk, which has been well scored over with initials and dates—one cut in that fatal year for the monarchy, 1649.

The Hospital at present contains five brothers and five sisters, who have comfortable rooms, and enjoy pensions amounting in value to a little over £30 each. A similar number of out brothers and sisters enjoy a pension of £25 each. Below the Refectory there is a fine crypt, which is very interesting as an example of transition from Norman to Early English. The round arches of the groined roof have the character of the former, while the round abaci of the pillars correspond to the latter style.

CHAPTER XI.

St. Mildred's Church.

T. Mildred's lies out of the beaten track, and is hidden away in an obscure part of the city which has long ceased to be the abode of the affluent; it is probable therefore that visitors to Canterbury often miss seeing it, and that many who have lived all their lives in the city have never entered this church, which is one of the most interesting in Canterbury.

As we pass through Stour Street it is sad to see the signs of squalid poverty which abound in the densely packed courts and alleys which lie between the street and the river. Here and there an old timber-framed house stands sound and sightly yet, in the midst of modern decay, though its foundations were laid two hundred years or more ago. But St. Mildred's was old St. Mildred's then, and although some part of its beauty has departed, we may be glad that in our own days a new reverence has grown up for the ancient fabrics which were reared in the dawn of our history, so that they are cared for and religiously preserved.

At what epoch a Christian church was first built where St. Mildred's now stands we know not, but the record of the stones antedates that of the historian. The walls of the church bear witness to an antiquity

S.W. quoin, St. Mildred's.

beyond that which arch and window would imply, and we do not doubt that here, as at St. Martin's, there has been a building of importance since the Roman times. Not only do Roman tiles abound in the walls, but there is strong reason to believe that the massive blocks of oolite which are built into the quoins of the south wall of the nave, were also taken from a Roman building. Mr. Hussey called attention to these stones in Vol. I. of *Archæologia Cantiana*. Since then the late Sir Gilbert Scott pointed out that the very peculiar coarse oolite of these blocks is exactly that of the Roman pillars from Reculver, which are now on the south side of Canterbury Cathedral. It is also of exactly the same kind as the large blocks found in the most ancient part of the old Saxon church at Dover Castle.

Gostling, writing a century ago, speaks of undoubted Roman remains still visible at St. Mildred's, and states that, in the pulling down of part of the city wall in 1769, the destroyers were stopped by a course of Roman brick, quite through the wall. He also speaks of "a fair Roman arch" over the window of the "west end of the south aisle." The "fair Roman arch," however, is no more than a pointed arch in which Roman bricks from an earlier building have been made use of. Gostling supposes that the Christians of the Roman garrison may have had a chapel at St. Mildred's. According to Stow, the church was destroyed by fire in 1246. That part of it was burnt is probable, but portions of the present fabric seem undoubtedly earlier than the date mentioned. The Rectory was an appanage of St. Augustine's Monastery, until the time of the dissolution, when it was taken by the King.

The church, at the present time, consists of a nave and chancel, each with its north aisle. A south chancel of the Tudor period has been converted into a south chapel by filling up its arch. A small north chapel opens into the chancel aisle, and is now used as a vestry. A tower formerly stood on the north side between the two north aisles, but this was pulled down, the materials of the tower and the fine peal of bells it contained being sold. The church is large and lofty, but its fine chancel would appear to still greater advantage if the south chancel were again opened, and the organ, which now blocks up the north aisle, placed therein. There is a remarkable variety in the pointed arches dividing the nave and the chancel from the north aisles. The two nearest the west end are alike, and very obtuse, the next is higher and more acute, while the chancel arcade is more pointed still. Mediæval architects were never slaves to symmetrical monotony; they adapted the lines of their work to the necessities of the situation, and no doubt that is sufficient explanation of the peculiar dissimilarity of these arches. The pillars supporting the nave arches are octagonal, each face slightly concaved, as are also the capitals and bases. On the westernmost pillar is a bracket and niche, with a rectangular canopy, once probably occupied by a statuette of the Madonna, or St. Mildred.

The windows are various in style; the five-light east window of the chancel has good rectilinear tracery; it is to be hoped some munificent churchman will one day give it its due adornment of painted glass. The west window, in the same style, is of three lights, and the south windows have elegant curvilinear tracery. In the aisle are five lancet windows, two of which are filled with stained glass. One is a memorial window "to James and Sarah Houlden, erected by their daughter, Mary Ann, September, 1881." The second has a mournful interest, as being the gift of the late Miss Pemell, who met with a tragical death in the fire on the Dane John. In one of the south windows is the only fragment of old glass in the church—a rude figure of St. Mildred.

The ceiling at the east end of the chancel is pannelled in wood; the carved oak bench heads of the stalls are interesting remnants of the ancient miserere stalls. The carved bird is possibly a rebus on the name of the ancient family of Cokyn. Another genuine relic of old wood carving is the font-cover. The stone font is octagonal, each panel bearing a quatrefoil.

The monuments are interesting, especially those to the Cranmers. The first of these is an elegant marble monument, painted and gilded, in memory of Thomas Cranmer, son of Edmund Cranmer. The latter was Archdeacon of Canterbury, and Provost of Wingham, and held various other preferments bestowed upon him by his brother, Archbishop Cranmer, but in 1554 he had to escape into Germany to save his life,

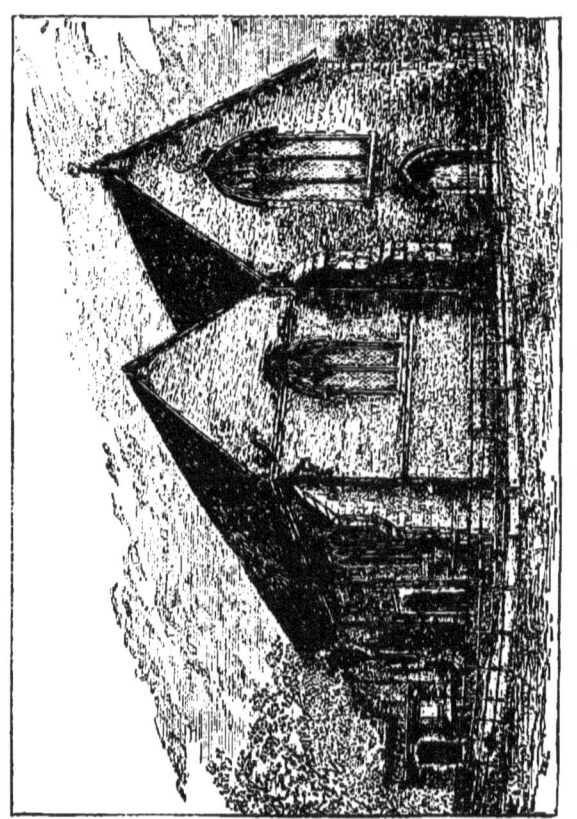

ST. MILDRED'S CHURCH (WEST END).

ST. MILDRED'S CHURCH.

being charged that he, a priest, had married. His preferments were taken from him, and he was enjoined to abandon his wife, but he refused to do so, and died many years after in Germany. His son, Thomas, whose tomb is in St. Mildred's, lived in that parish, was a charitable and worthy citizen, and died in 1604, aged 69.

Old Bench-head, St. Mildred's.

Another monument is to the memory of Sir William Cranmer, Knt., a descendant also of Edmund Cranmer. In 1691, he was chosen governor of the Merchant Adventurers Company, London. He died in 1697, but was not buried at St. Mildred's.

The numerous mural, and other memorials of departed worthies, once resident in St. Mildred's, remind us that the parish had its fair share, in former days, of wealthy parishioners. One tablet commemorates "Thomassine Honywood, widowe, late ye wife of Antiony Honywood of this Pishe, Esq., and before ye wife of John Adye, of Doddington, 9th July, 1626. One of her sons married Elizabeth Waller, eldest daughter of Thos. Waller of *Beckonsfield*, in the county of Buck." In the chancel aisle is a handsome marble monument to various members of the Bridger family. Here also, concealed by the organ, is an altar tomb of Sir Francis Head, Bart., who died 1716. Close by is a memorial tablet, dated 1844, to John Cooper, "Alderman and Magistrate of this city for 30 years, and during that time, three times elected to the important office of Mayor."

The churchyard contains one monument, which the citizens ought, out of gratitude, to take under their charge. It is the tomb of worthy Alderman Simmons, who, at the beginning of the present century, converted what was then known as the Dane John Field, into a beautiful garden and recreation ground for the citizens. This he did at a cost of £1,500. We read on his monument (which much needs some "Old Mortality's" loving hand to set it in order) that—"The many services which he rendered to his native city, added to the extraordinary ability that he possessed, so raised him in the estimation of his fellow citizens, that they, with one voice, conferred on him the honour of a seat in Parliament, the important duties of which it pleased God he should but a very short time fulfil. Death rendered the motto of his arms 'Vincit qui patitur,' of no further avail." The Alderman died in 1807. Close to his grave is that of Capon Weekes, the father of a distinguished son—Henry Weekes, R.A., of whose memory, as a native genius, Canterbury should feel proud. On other tombs around, we read the brief records of many notable Canterbury families who formerly resided in this parish.

The exterior of St. Mildred's is worthy of attention and study, the remarkable south wall of the nave especially, in which flint, Roman tiles and oolitic stones are mingled. It is evidently the most ancient part of the church. The south chancel is a curious example of the chequered flint work so much fancied in the Tudor period. There is a rough cross, shaped in flints, in the west wall. In the east wall of the chancel there is another cross of elegant design, carved in low relief, on a stone tablet. The south chancel was erected by Thomas Attwood, who lived in Stour Street, in the time of Henry VIII., and was four times Mayor of Canterbury. He and several of his family were buried in it, but their monuments have disappeared.

We were anxious to ascertain some account of the tower, and the Rector (Dr. Mangan) kindly sought among the archives of the church the faculty obtained for its destruction. This informs us that, at a meeting of the vestry, on 25th June, 1832, it was resolved the tower should be pulled down, to make room for additional sittings "for the poor parishioners," and that four of the five bells should be sold, the remaining one being "sufficient for the necessary uses of the said parish." A sum of £101 6s. had been raised in the parish. This, with the price obtained for the bells, was to be devoted to the necessary alterations. Two bells were inscribed Richard Phelps, 1711, one "Josephus Hatch mee fecit 1622." Another dated 1536 had a figure of Christ, bound, and wearing the crown of thorns, and an inscription in old English—"I.H.S. Have marce on the soules of Thomas Wood, and Margaret his wyfe."

With the Rectory of St. Mildred's is united that of St. Mary de Castro. This latter church has long since been destroyed. Somner, speaking of "St. Mary Castle," says—"this Church hath lyen long desolate; and the chancel only is left standing of it. Time was, it was as absolute a Parish Church as any about the city." The chancel ruins have long since disappeared, and only the name of the Church survives in St. Mary Street. St. Mary of the Castle had at an earlier period absorbed the adjacent small parish of St. John the Poor. This church stood at the end of St. John's Lane, and Somner speaks of its having been "of a long time prophaned into a malt-house or the like."

CHAPTER XII.

St. Margaret's, St. George's, St. Mary Magdalen's and St. Paul's.

HE Church of St. Margaret is not architecturally noteworthy. It formerly consisted of a nave and chancel, with two aisles and two chancel-chapels. Somner says that the south chapel was dedicated to St. John, and the other to "Our Lady." The chapel of St. John was sliced off, and the east end of the church deformed, in order to straighten the street. The deformity was skilfully masked by the late Sir Gilbert Scott in the restoration carried out during the incumbency of the Rev. E. H. Woodall. The wall of the south chancel was set back and an apse erected. The fine organ, which fills up the irregular space in the north aisle, was the gift of Mr. Woodall, who contributed most generously to the cost of the restoration, and devoted a very considerable sum to the adornment of the church.

The three aisles are separated by arcades of pointed arches on octagonal pillars. The small belfry-tower at the west end of the south aisle contains three bells, one dated 1599, and two by Hatch dated 1625. The Baptistery under the tower has been recently paved with tiles. Reverent care has been devoted to the adornment of the church throughout; its decorations and fittings are in good taste, and several of the windows have been filled with stained glass. The most imposing monument is that of Sir George Newman, whose recumbent figure is carved in marble. He was a Judge of the Cinque Ports, and Commissary of Archbishops Whitgift, Bancroft, and Abbot. High up on the south wall, almost out of sight, is a bust of John Watson, a worthy citizen of Canterbury, who filled the several offices of Mayor, Chamberlain, and Sheriff, and in 1633 left property to be applied to the purchase of "good russett cloth gowns" to be given to the "most miserable, poorest, aged, blind, impotent and decrepit." The bust was originally in the chancel. The most notable of those whom we know to have had their last resting-place in this church was William Somner, the learned author of the "Antiquities of Canterbury," to whose memory there is a small brass wall tablet. Somner wrote his great book during the reign of Charles I., and published it under the patronage of Archbishop Laud, in 1640. In that same year, as Batteley tells us, "a dismal storm did arise, which did shake and threaten with a final overthrow, the very foundation of the Church. The madness of the people did rage, and prevailed beyond resistance. The venerable Dean and Canons were turned out of their stalls, * * * and whatsoever there was of beauty or decency in the Holy Place, was despoiled by the outrages of Sacrilege and Prophaneness." At such a time the work of so thorough a churchman as Somner was ill-timed, and "the best fate which the book or its author could at that time expect, was to lie hid, and to be sheltered under the security of being not regarded." Laud fell; the King fell; Cromwell passed away; the Commonwealth came to an end; and the Restoration found Somner still living, and his book unsold. In 1662 the publisher printed a new title page, bearing that year's date, and the work was sold. Somner thought of issuing a second edition, but died, in 1669, before he could carry out his design.

Among the noted parishioners of St. Margaret's was a certain John Winter, who, in 1470, left two tenements at the "Yren Cross," of the value of sixteen shillings annually, to pay the cost of a lamp to burn continually before the High Altar. The Iron Cross spoken of stood at the junction of Watling Street and St. Margaret's Street. The two houses left by John Winter were confiscated to the Crown when lamp burning before altars came to be considered superstitious; they were purchased by Alderman Watson, above referred to, and were left by him for the poor of the city. John Winter was buried in the chancel of the church. Leonard Cotton, Mayor in 1579, the founder of Cotton's Hospital, was also buried in St. Margaret's.

An Ecclesiastical Court, which was established in 1560, held its sittings in the Chapel of the Virgin. There the Archbishop of Canterbury held his quadrennial visitation of the clergy of this part of the diocese. In this church also till very recently, the Archdeacons of Canterbury have held their annual visitations. The living is a rectory; it was one of the many benefices attached to the Abbey of St. Augustine; but in 1271 it was transferred to the Poor Priests' Hospital. Since 1586, however, it has been in the gift of the Archdeacons of Canterbury.

* * * *

 FEW years ago St. George's Church underwent extensive alterations and enlargement, to accommodate the parishioners of the united parishes of St. George and St. Mary Magdalen. Some portion however of the ancient structure remains. It was one of the churches attached to Christ Church, and when the Monastery was dissolved, the rectory was transferred to the Dean and Chapter. The original church consisted of a nave and south aisle. It had formerly a steeple extending into the street, the footpath passing through an arch in the tower, but this was taken down towards the end of the last century. There is in the north wall a small closed-up doorway, which, no doubt, formerly gave access to the steeple. The church, as it now stands, consists of a nave and chancel, with north and south aisles. The chancel and the north aisle are new, having been erected during the recent restoration of the church, which was due to the energy and zeal of the late Rector (the Rev. N. H. McGachen).

The nave and aisles are separated by arcades of five pointed arches on octagonal pillars, with square abaci. Three of the pillars on the

ST. GEORGE'S CHURCH.

north side were brought from old Burgate Church. The others, which are new, have been made to correspond in style. The tower is supported on pointed arches. Access to the belfry and clock-chamber is obtained from the gallery. In the south wall is a tomb recess, and a piscina of early date. In the east end of this south aisle, is a three light window, to the memory of Mrs. Kingsford, who died in 1841. The altar formerly stood below this window. In the south wall, at this end, are two sedilia; an ancient door, now blocked up, was probably a priest's door. In the floor of the nave is a brass, with the figure of John Lovelle, priest, rector of the church, who died 1438. A tombstone, partly broken, bears an inscription to Villai Dole, minister of the French church, in 1686. The north aisle contains a three light window to the memory of the Hon. Mrs. Isaac, who died in St. George's parish in 1850.

The font is ancient and curious, octagonal, supported on a central pedestal and *seven* surrounding pillars. There was formerly, at the east end of the church, on a panel of wood, a painting representing Guy Fawkes entering the Parliament House. It bore a latin inscription showing that it had been placed there "to perpetuate the memory of popish infamy." It was apparently painted during the reign of Charles I. The Registers of the church, which date from 1574, contain a copy of the entries of a previous Register, dating back to 1538.

* * * *

HE living of St. Mary Magdalen, Burgate, was united to that of St. George's in 1681, and the former church was pulled down in 1871. The tower remains still standing. It is recorded that Sir Harry Ramsey, of St. George's parish, gave six seams of lime towards the rebuilding of it in 1503. A few monuments are preserved under the tower, one being to an extraordinary Canterbury character, Betty Bolaine, the miser, who was buried in the church in 1805. The church contained incised brasses, which "disappeared" during the process of demolition. Two of these, the oldest figured brasses in Canterbury, were in memory of Christopher

Klook, and his wife Margareta. The earliest bore date 1494. The church had a Norman font, which was sold, we believe, to a church near Dover. The ancient bells were also sold. One is in St. George's Church, and two went to Madagascar. In a house close to the church "Tom Ingoldsby" (Rev. R. H. Barham) the author of the "Ingoldsby Legends," was born. William Gray, a relative of Stephen Gray, the first discoverer of electrical conduction, was buried in this church in 1714. He had been sixty years in the city Council.

* * * *

ASTED speaks of St. Paul's as a small mean building, but much has been done, since his day, to enlarge and beautify the church. Its pointed arches and round pillars are Early English, but the oldest windows belong to the late pointed style. There are three piscinas in the chancel and the north aisle; the roof is pannelled; the tower contains three bells. In the reign of Henry III. the Rectory of the parish belonged to Hamo Doge, who endowed the Vicarage and founded the Chantry, of which the name survives in Chantry Lane. The living was settled by Henry VIII. on his new Dean and Chapter, and remained with them until its union with St. Martin's in 1681. It was then arranged that the presentation should alternately be made by the Archbishop and the Dean and Chapter. The church had no burial ground of its own, and the parishioners used that of St. Augustine's Abbey until 1591, when the ground in Longport was purchased and consecrated. There is a brass tablet on the chancel wall in memory of John Twyne, a worthy schoolmaster, who, in the reign of Queen Elizabeth, taught the boys Latin, and ruled the city as Mayor. He died in 1581. A tombstone in the north aisle bears an inscription on a brass plate—" Sacred to the never dyeing memory of the much bemoand and lamented patterne of all goodness, George Fineux, Esq., gent, second sonne to Thomas Fineux, Esq., of Huttam, who changed this mortall life the 24th October, A.D. 1653."

In this parish died in 1737 David Fferne, a noted dwarf. The

ST. PAUL'S CHURCH. 77

parish Register records that "David Fferne, the short man, born in the shire of Ross, in the parish of Fferne, aged 27 years, was but 30 inches from head to foot, and 36 inches about." A mural monument records the loyalty and the reward thereof of Sir William Rooke—"After some years' imprisonment, and other sufferings," during the Commonwealth, he was, soon after the Restoration (1660), given a regiment of foot, and the command of a troop of horse, with other proofs of Royal gratitude. Sir William's seat was at St. Lawrence, Canterbury, at which he lived and died. Here too lived his more distinguished son, Admiral Sir George Rooke, who did good service in driving out the next Sovereign of that Stuart line, to which his father had been so devoted. William III. promoted him to the rank of rear admiral of the red, and his capture of Gibraltar in 1704, won for him a deathless fame in English history. Queen Ann received him with all honour, but he retired, still in the prime of life, to spend a few years in his quiet home at Canterbury, where he died in 1708, and was buried in St. Paul's church. Still another Rooke is connected with the traditions of St. Paul's, having fought a fatal duel in the North Holmes with Ensign Buckeridge. Both were killed. A stone, on which the words "Rooke died here" are barely legible, still marks the spot.

The enlargement of St. Paul's Church is due to the late Rev. W. J. Chesshyre, M.A., for 17 years rector of St. Martin's with St. Paul's. To his memory the handsome west window was erected by public subscription in 1859. The south aisle was erected by him, and other extensive improvements carried out. The chancel was enlarged and a new four-light east window with good Decorated tracery and painted glass, was erected to the memory of William Henry Furley, Esq. A handsome new reredos has recently been placed below it. The north aisle also contains a new three-light east window. The chancel has a memorial window to the Rev. W. A. Newman, formerly Dean of Cape Town, and in the new south aisle is a window to the late Mr. John Lancefield. The font is new, and replaced an ancient one, the square basin of which stood on four marble columns. Joseph Hatch, the celebrated founder of bells, was married at St. Paul's in 1607.

CHAPTER XIII.

St. Stephen's, Hackington.

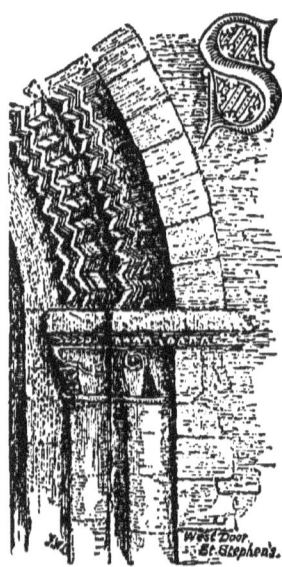

West Door,
St. Stephen's.

T. STEPHEN'S, Hackington, is situated about a mile from the centre of the city, on the north. It is a charming spot, with the old church half hidden amidst surrounding circles of limes, the quaint cluster of cottages and almshouses, the fine mansion of Hales Place, the park with its timbered background of hill, the village school, the adjacent farm, and the 'Beverley,' whose ancient host has catered to his rustic neighbours for three score years, and has officiated as parish-clerk over three generations of them, from baptism to burial, ever since George the Third was King.

We must go back to the days of Stephen Langton for the origin of the intimate connection of the church with the Archdeacons of Canterbury. The great Archbishop who had so large a share in the struggle between King John and the Barons, attached the living of Hackington to the Archdeaconry then held by his brother Simon. This Simon Langton had taken a notable part against John; he had been an active partizan of the French Dauphin, who made him his Chancellor. It is not surprising therefore that by the time John's son Henry had grown to manhood, Simon had grown "not only out of means, but also out of favour both with the King and Pope." It was then, however, that Stephen Langton, remembering that " charity begins at home," provided handsomely for his brother by making him Archdeacon of Canterbury, and giving him the livings of St. Stephen's and Teynham. Simon removed to the vicarage of Hackington, which long continued to be the residence of the Archdeacons, who had previously occupied a small house in St. Gregory's. He founded the Poor Priests' Hospital at Canterbury, and died in 1248, having held the archdeaconry for twenty-one years. Matthew Paris, the monk, says of him that, having upset the peace of two kingdoms, it was not wonderful that he became a perturber and persecutor of his Church at Canterbury. Hackington, as the residence of the Archdeacons of Canterbury during three centuries, must have been the home of many distinguished men—whether of Archdeacon Peter Roger, who became Pope Gregory XI., we know not. It was there that Archbishops Arundel and Warham died. It narrowly missed becoming a more important place. Archbishop Baldwin, who went with Cœur de Lion to the Crusades, and died in the Holy Land, began to build a college for secular canons at Hackington, but it was never completed, for the monks of Christ Church, with their Prior Alan, appealed to the Pope against the scheme, and a bull was issued commanding the Archbishop to pull down what he had erected.

Hackington can boast of a connection with royalty. Edward III. held a tilt there on his return from the French war. Henry VI. had a house and park there; these in the reign of Elizabeth were granted to Sir Roger Manwood. This worthy barrister, who became Chief Baron of the Exchequer, was a great benefactor to St. Stephen's, and founded the almshouses which serve to perpetuate his memory in the village. His mansion, which adjoined the churchyard, was no doubt the former residence of the archdeacons; it remained in the Manwood family till 1637, when the estate was sold to Colonel Colepepper. In 1675 Mr. E. Hales became the owner of it; he was knighted by James II., and it was his great grandson, Sir Edward Hales, Bart., who pulled down the

ST. STEPHEN'S CHURCH.

old mansion and built, on the slope of the hill, the fine house which has recently been so greatly altered and enlarged for St. Mary's Jesuit College.

The church is beautifully situated at the base of the hill, and is surrounded by rows of splendid lindens. It is cruciform in shape, the massively buttressed tower at the west end being equal in breadth to the nave. The west door is a most valuable example of the transition from the Norman, to which style its mouldings and capitals belong, but the arch is pointed. Through this door we enter into the belfry, from which a rather curious carved oak door leads into the nave. Over it is the date, 1630, and the text, "Let all things be done decently and in order." The tower contains eight bells, which are sweet toned and melodious. The St. Stephen's ringers have a reputation to maintain, and are not unmindful to place on record their efforts in the delightful art of change-ringing. A tablet tells us that the two trebles were added to the peal in 1845, when Holt's ten-part peal of 5040 grandsire triples was rung by the St. Stephen's Amateur Society in three hours and one minute. Another tablet records that in 1847 there was rung a true and complete peal of 6720 Bob-Major changes in four hours and three minutes.

Within the south porch is a well preserved Norman doorway; the head of the arch is filled in with diapered squares, and the shafts have cushion capitals. This doorway, a nave window near it, and the lower parts of the tower are the only portions of the church which retain Norman characteristics. The nave windows, with the one exception mentioned, are pointed, some lancets. The chancel arch is pointed, but the transept arches round. The chancel is large in proportion to the nave. It is well lighted by a handsome east window of five lights, the tracery perpendicular. The windows north and south of the chancel are very elegant; their tracery is apparently late Decorated merging into Perpendicular. The north transept has a three light window which is worthy of notice, but the other windows are without interest. The chancel screen is carved oak. The stone font was presented by Sir Roger Manwood in 1591.

K

The most noteworthy of the monuments is that of Sir Roger Manwood in the south transept. It is of marble, and contains in a central niche a fine bust of the knight in his costume as Chief Baron of the Exchequer. In panels below are kneeling marble figures of his first wife Dorothy and their five children; on the other side kneels his second wife Elizabeth, without offspring. On the slab of the tomb, upon an admirably carved pallet of plaited rush, lies the effigy of Sir Roger in grim and bony nakedness. The skeleton is a clever work of wood-carving. Above the tomb are suspended a helmet, sword, and gloves, presumably those of Sir Roger, though his weapons were probably such as the arm of the law might wield. A Latin inscription tells us that, amongst his other good works, he founded Sandwich School. He died in 1592.

This monument of Sir Roger Manwood is of greater interest to the archæologist than a casual observer would expect. The bust of the Chief Baron bears the famous "collar of SS," which has engaged the pens of so many antiquarians. The collar is so named from certain links shaped like the letter S. The interest arises as to what that letter signifies and what was the origin of this particular collar, evidently a badge of great distinction. Whether the S stands for the martyred Simplicius; or for the name of the Countess of Salisbury, whose garter became historical; for "Soverayne," the motto of Henry IV., or for "Souvenez," a supposed motto of his noble father, "time-honoured Lancaster," which are some of the many explanations given, it is not for us to decide. It was undoubtedly worn by Henry IV. and by his Queen. It has passed through stages of development; and it is still a collar of SS that is worn by the Lord Chief Justice. Sir Roger Manwood was, it seems, the first of the Lord Chief Barons to receive the honoured decoration, the use of which was limited by special statute in the reign of Henry VIII. The Latin epitaph records the chief points in the career of Sir Roger, who died in December, 1592. It is curious that the thirteen lines, commencing—

"Inclines oculum me conspice marmore pressum"

are also quoted by Parsons as graven on a tombstone, dated 1436, in

Graveney Church, to John Martyn, who was a Judge in the time of Henry VI.

On the wall of the nave, near the south door, is a beautiful epitaph, written by Sir John Manwood, in memory of his wife, 20th May, 1642. It is a touching record of a true and noble woman. The first part of the inscription is as follows:—"Glory be to God on High, our Most Gracious Saviour! Within this Church (the temple of the everlasting God) lies the body of Lievina, Lady Manwood, in the vault belonging to my family. She was eldest daughter to Sir John Ogle, Knt., sometime a Colonel in the Netherlands and Governor of Utrecht, where he was in martial affairs and at home in England, both in his life and death justly preclare. She was a most indulgent wife to me from the very hour of our happy and blessed conjunction in marriage, which was on the 11th December, 1627, till the 19th February, 1641, in the evening of which day, between 9 and 10 o'clock, we were separated by her dissolution and my recovery out of a dangerous sickness. In the extremity whereof grief so possessed and pierced through her most pious heart that she instantly sickened, and died five days after, in the 36th year of her age. Her life was most pious and full of charity; her conversation sweet, most sweetly discreet; for she flattered none, yet obliged all. Her love to me was most singularly true and eminent; and as God's priest united us sacredly in marriage, so God Himself did our hearts and souls, for we had but one heart and one soul: death hath separated our bodies, but can never our souls. For hers is praising God in Heaven, and so doth mine, though my body is on the Earth. Death and the Resurrection will unite again our souls and bodies eternally to praise our God, the most Glorious Trinity—which God of His infinite mercy grant."

The north transept contains the memorials of the Baker family, long intimately associated with St. Stephen's, and on the wall of the nave are monuments to other members of the same family, whose present representative is W. de Chair Baker, Esq., of St. Stephen's. One is to the memory of Colonel Charles Cyril Taylor, C.B., who was killed at Sobraon. He was the eldest son of Lieut.-Col. Taylor (who was killed at Vimiera) and Elizabeth, daughter of the late John Baker, formerly M.P. for Canterbury.

The chancel east window is filled with stained glass, representing our Saviour and the Four Evangelists. It was the gift of the late Rev. John White, who was Vicar of the parish for 39 years. The chancel contains a memorial of "Captain William Alcock, Esquire, who served his country faithfully, both by sea and land, lived virtuously, and on 21st February, 1616, ended his life most Christianly in sure hope to rise again." On the south side of the chancel is a painted window (Christ and the Woman of Samaria) by Willement, which, with a handsome brass, is "in memory of John Furley, of Canterbury, Banker, born 5th April, 1773, died 7th November, 1854."

Close to the Church are the almshouses of Manwood's Hospital, six single houses, the seventh (a double house) the abode of the parish clerk. The present occupant (Edward Austen) has held the office for 63 years, and is one of the very few certificated parish clerks remaining in the kingdom. He was one of the ringers of the two peals alluded to above, and still takes his place in the octave with as much spirit, if not as much strength, as he did half a century back. The patronage of the almshouses is attached to the ownership of the Hales' Estate.

CHAPTER XIV.

St. Dunstan's Church.

HE Church of St. Dunstan's is one of the most interesting of the parish churches of Canterbury. It is outside the ancient boundaries of the city, but it has long been brought practically within it. It was one of the many foundations of Archbishop Lanfranc (1070-1089), who made it an appanage of his Priory of St. Gregory in Northgate.

A hundred years passed away, and St. Dunstan's formed a stage in the pilgrimage of the King of England to the shrine of Becket. Henry had dismounted at Harbledown, and walked with his attendants to St. Dunstan's. Entering the church, the king partly stripped, put on the hair shirt and the cloak of the pilgrim, and walked barefooted to the Cathedral. The little Norman Church became, no doubt, a place of some note in connection with the king's penance. Other pilgrims would be likely to follow Henry's example, and pause at St. Dunstan's before passing on their way into the city. By whom the church of Lanfranc was enlarged we cannot say, but the vicarage was established and endowed by Archbishop Reynolds in 1322, and during the same century, one Henry of Canterbury, a chaplain of the king, founded a chapel on the north side of the church, dedicating it to the Holy Trinity. He endowed there a perpetual chantry, which he gave in charge to the Poor Priest's Hospital. This chantry was continued until the Reformation. It was not the only one, however, attached to the church, for we read that two chaplains were maintained by the Roper family to sing masses at the altar of St. Nicholas, for the souls of their dead. This family, during several centuries, lived in the parish, and were buried in the church. It was a Roper who built the chancel aisle, known as the Roper Chancel. The family residence was at Place House, or St. Dunstan's Place, which stood opposite the churchyard, its site being at present occupied by the brewery of Messrs. Flint and Sons. Only the old gateway of the mansion remains (see initial). One William Rosper, who resided there in the reign of Henry III., was a great benefactor to St. Martin's Priory, Dover. The Ropers continued to be buried in the church till the elder male line became extinct, but their vault continued to receive members of the family down to 1741. Lord Teynham, a Roper-Curzon, is descended from a Christopher Roper, of the 16th century.

The chantries and masses, with their attendant friars, were swept away at the Reformation, but that same period furnished to the church a relic which is still preserved in it—the decapitated head of Sir Thomas More. The sturdy Chancellor preferred to accept death rather than acknowledge Henry VIII. to be the supreme head of the church. He was executed on Tower Hill in 1535. His body was first buried in the tower, and afterwards in Chelsea church. His head, as usual in such cases, was set up on a pole on London Bridge. There it remained for a fortnight, when his daughter Margaret obtained possession of it, and having encased the head in a leaden casket treasured it as a precious relic till her death. Margaret More married John Roper, and spent her last days at St. Dunstan's. She was buried in the Roper vault, where her leaden coffin was found intact a few years since. At her earnest desire the head of her father was buried in the vault. It was placed within a grated niche in the wall, and there remains to the present day.

St. Dunstan's Church: North side.

St. Dunstan's, like most of our churches, shows the work of several ages. During the recent restoration the plaster having been removed from the exterior, some ancient "herring-bone" flint work was laid bare in the north wall; this was probably a part of Lanfranc's original structure. The present entrance to the church is by the north porch, erected in the reign of the second James. From this a door opens into the Trinity Chapel which is now used as a vestry. The original external doorway of the chapel has been blocked up, but it can still be seen. The chapel contains a well preserved piscina and a "squint," now closed, through which when the "poor priests" chanted mass the altar of the Trinity Chapel could be seen from the church.

The church consists of a nave, with a south aisle, and a chancel which has a south aisle known as the Roper Chancel. Four pointed arches, with elegant moulded piers and circular shafts, divide the nave from the aisle. The nave and aisle windows have good tracery; the west window is later, but good. There is a trefoiled lancet in the chancel, and a square-headed, two-light window filled with stained glass, "in memory of Edward and Sarah Holttum, erected by their only surviving son, Charles Holttum, F.R.C.S.E." The east window of three lights with good tracery, contains small painted medallions. There appears to be no old glass in the church. Two pointed arches with an octagonal pillar, separate the chancel from the Roper chancel; the latter has a flat timber ceiling, panelled. It contains two ancient altar tombs of Bethersden marble, monuments of the Ropers, once richly carved, but now in a sad state of decay. Their brasses have been stolen. Below this chancel is the Roper vault above referred to. A monument to the son of Margaret Roper is now on the north wall; it was formerly in this chancel. There are no other monuments of any note, but several quaint old tombstones cover the now filled up vaults. One in the south aisle commemorates Claude Rondeau, a "marchant" at Canterbury. "refugee in England for the Protestant religion." Several of the Rondeau family were buried there. The father died in 1720. One son died at St. Petersburg, after living there nine years as His Majesty's Resident (1739).

Near this is a curious memorial of "Elizabeth Scranton, who, having lived a vertuous and pious life, died ye sixth day of February, in the 47th yeare of her virginity, and of man's salvation 1685." Other old tombstones commemorate Christopher Browne, who died 1657, and Daniel Hall, who was twice Mayor of Canterbury; his first wife was Leah Rigden, who died in 1703. The tower at the west end of the south aisle contains a belfry with six bells. Below it is an octagonal font, with an oak cover of elaborate tabernacle work.

In a field opposite to the church once stood a chapel, built by Archbishop Baldwin in 1187, and dedicated to Thomas à Becket. A fair used annually to be held in St. Dunstan's. The parish once also enjoyed two privileges which it would scarcely desire to recover—a prison and a gallows, the former in St. Dunstan's Street, the latter on St. Thomas's Hill.

CHAPTER XV.

Holy Cross, Westgate; St. Peter's; St. Alphege; St. Mary Northgate; and other Churches.

OLY Cross, Westgate, was erected by Archbishop Sudbury about 500 years ago. It replaced the church which stood over the former Westgate, and which was pulled down when the Archbishop rebuilt a part of the city wall and erected the present Westgate. The church consists of a nave, chancel, and two aisles; it has a square tower at the south west corner. Formerly a porch and chantry stood where the road now intervenes between the church and the Westgate. Over the porch anciently stood a sculptured representation of the Crucifixion—with Mary and John at the foot of the Cross. In a will dated 1521, Richard Marley instructed his executors "to see gilt well and workmanly the Crucifix of our Lord." The Crucifix, however, had disappeared by Somner's time, and had been replaced by the King's Arms. There was anciently a priest's room over the porch, for the accommodation no doubt of the priest of the "Jesus Masse," who was maintained by the "Fraternity of the Jesus Masse, with the help and devotion of the parishioners." This Chantry was supported by lands and tenements in St. Dunstan's and Harbledown. The priest's stipend, including costs of wax and wine, amounted to £7 a year, the parish clerk having 6s. 8d. for ringing to the said mass, and helping to sing it. The Fraternity was dissolved in the time of Edward VI. Holy Cross was frequently used

L

for the performance of the "Miracle Plays" so common in the middle ages.

The church has probably undergone considerable alterations since its erection; the present tower dates only from a few years since, the old structure having become unsafe; it contains five bells. No trace of the old chantry now remains, the site having been taken up in making the new road. Close to the spot on which this chantry stood there was buried the last criminal executed at Westgate. A few aged citizens still remember seeing Nicholas Nolan hanged there for highway robbery on the Sturry Road. The church is spacious but architecturally of no great interest. The windows are either late Decorated or Perpendicular. The chancel contains a three-light pointed east window and two square headed windows on each side. It has a few old carved oak miserere stalls, and there is a piscina in the south wall. It also contains a mural monument to Deane John Parker, who died 1838, aged 72 years. Below this is a memorial to Robert Deane, "a man of meek and humble manners and unostentatious piety." We are told that a Sunday School which he founded in this parish, together with a gallery and organ erected at his own expense, remain to perpetuate his memory. But gallery and organ have already disappeared. Mr. Deane died in 1808 at the ripe age of 90. There is a monument to James Six, M.A., Fellow of Trinity College, Cambridge, who died at Rome, 1786, aged 62, Canterbury being his native place. The Six family were descended, we believe, from a celebrated Burgomaster of Amsterdam. Into the tower has been shifted the monumental bust of Abraham Colfe, a worthy whose name and fame are all but forgotten in his native city. He died in 1656, and left his estate to the Leather Sellers' Company, of which he was a member, directing, by his will, that 27s. yearly should be paid to the minister of "Rood Church," near the Westgate, to be spent in distributing bread to the poor. The font is octagonal, on a shaft of similar form; the carved wood cover is an elaborate specimen of tabernacle work.

Holy Cross originally belonged to the Priory of St. Gregory. The vicarage was endowed by Archbishop Stratford in 1347. It was united

ST. PETER'S CHURCH.

with the rectory of St. Peter in 1681, by Archbishop Sancroft. The patronage is alternately vested in the Archbishop and the Dean and Chapter.

* * * *

THE old Church of St. Peter in the High Street is rarely entered, and has ceased to be used for Divine Service, although an occasional marriage is solemnised there. It is in a shocking state of disrepair and dirt, and owing to many years of gross neglect is rapidly becoming a ruin. It is a most singularly irregular building; the nave has a decided curve, and narrows from east to west; the south aisle is very narrow, the north aisle very broad. The nave is separated from the aisles by arcades of pointed arches, which all vary in size and are not regular in position. There is no chancel arch, but the piers of the arcades at the east end are pierced on either side; on the north by a low feathered ogee arch within the side of which there is a small square recess, probably an aumbry; on the south by a splayed lancet opening. The arches of the nave are pointed, without mouldings, mostly on square piers; on the north side there is one square pillar with square abacus. The arch and pier edges are chamfered. The middle pier on the south side has a pointed arch, high up. It is now filled up, but was evidently open to both nave and aisle. It is clear that the west end of the church and the north aisle have been much altered from the original building. It appears as if there had been at one time a chapel or baptistery at this end where is now the vestry; a north door opens to a bay of the aisle which is evidently much older than the curiously shaped extension of the aisle at that end. In this bay the aisle arch is pointed, the nave arch round. The tower at the south west corner has a small trefoiled window in the lower part, and later pointed windows in the belfry. The masonry of the tower indicates an early date, and then a reconstruction from material of a previous building. In its quoins are some unusually massive oolite stones not unlike those of St. Mildred's, and mixed with the flints of the walls are many apparently Roman tiles. The south door was originally handsomely arched, with shafts and carved capitals, a fragment of which remains on one side. There was no lack of doors to the church, for there are two more on the north side and one, hooded and moulded, in the east wall of the north aisle. These doors can only be properly seen from the churchyard outside, where it is not too safe to venture, for a vault occasionally caves in, and the centre buttress of the north aisle is ready to fall. The condition of the church on this side is most dangerous. Some of the windows are pointed, with fairly good tracery, others square and poor, and one "modern" pointed, hideous. A square window in the north aisle has elegant tracery, containing some fragments of good old glass. There is an old square font. The pulpit has an elaborate sounding board carved with cherubs, flowers, fruit, &c. Under the west window is a grand state pew with a painted back and canopy.

* * * *

T. Alphege, St. Alphage, or St. Elphege, for the name is variously spelt by both ancient and modern writers, is one of the oldest of the parish churches of Canterbury. It is dedicated to the Saxon Archbishop whom the Danes in their sack of the city in 1011 barbarously murdered. It is the only city church which was not at some time in the patronage of either St. Augustine's or Christ Church Abbeys. It has so long suffered neglect both within and without that it is now in a like condition to St. Peter's. It is doubtful if the fabric is safe; the tower is cracked, and not long since a part of its parapet fell into the churchyard. The interior of the church has not for many years been in a fit or decent state for Divine Worship; but recently an effort has been made to improve the condition of the church, and to infuse new life into the services, so that a marked improvement has taken place. The church has two aisles, the chancel being continuous with the south aisle. Five pointed arches on octagonal pillars separate the aisles; the roof has

tie-beams and king-posts. The tower is square, plain and low, and stands at the west end of the north aisle. It serves as a porch to the church, the principal entrance being by a doorway of the Tudor period. There is also a west door opening to the churchyard, and a south door in the chancel. The windows, most of which are Perpendicular, are but poor, with the exception of the two-light Decorated windows on the south side. The font is octagonal, and of the Tudor period, the panels bearing roses and shields. Fragments of old glass remain in some of the windows. On the second pillar is an inscription "Laude Prude Thoma per quem fit ista columptna." By his will, dated 1468, this Thomas Prude left money to erect a pillar in St. Alphege church, and from this the age of the greater part of the present building may be inferred. The most noteworthy parishioner buried in the church was John Caxton, a mercer, who died in 1483; he was brother of William Caxton, the first English printer.

* * * *

LD Northgate Church, or St. Mary Northgate, stood in part over an archway which formed the north gate of the city. It was removed and for the most part re-built. The north side of the old Norman church, however, remains in the present building, which is devoid of architectural interest. It has a remarkable brass of one Ralph Brown, who was Mayor of Canterbury in 1507 and during part of 1510. His epitaph is certainly a remarkable sample of spelling:—

> All ye that stand up on mi corse
> Rembember but lat Raff Brown I was
> All dyr man and Mayer of this cete
> Jesus a pon mi sowll have pete.

It was at Northgate that the Recorder of the City, with the Mayor, Aldermen, and other civic dignitaries, used to meet the King when passing through the city on his journey from Margate to London. At such times the ceremony of delivering up the keys of the city to the Sovereign was carried out with various loyal and flattering speeches from the Recorder, as the mouthpiece of the citizens.

* * * *

LITTLE need be said of the remaining city churches, for they contain scarcely anything to interest a visitor. St. Mary Bredman was so called it is said from a bread market which formerly stood next to it. The church is a plain oblong building without arches or divisions whatever. The adjoining Church House has a somewhat curious window looking into the church. The sister church, St. Andrew's, was only built in 1763-4, and has now ceased to be used. Old St. Andrew's stood in the centre of the street at what is now the Parade. In it was buried, in 1592, the Rev. Thos. Swift, rector of the parish for 22 years, and in 1624 his son Wm. Swift, rector for 33 years. The latter was also for 22 years rector of Harbledown. He was the great-grandfather of the celebrated Dean Swift. St. Mary Bredin's is an entirely new church, erected in 1866; it replaced a small Norman church which was built by a grandson of a certain Vitalis, who came into England with the Conqueror. In the old church were buried several of the Chiches, of the Donjon Manor, and members of the Hales family, who at a later date held that manor. All Saints' Church is also a modern church without a single feature calling for observation. It replaced an ancient church, the tower of which projected into the street. A beam crossing from the steeple to the opposite side of the road bore a large square clock in the centre.

CHAPTER XVI.

The Castle, City Walls, and Gates.

Tower of the city wall, Dane John.

DOMESDAY Book records that Canterbury Castle was given to the Conqueror by the Archbishop and the Abbot of St. Augustine's, in exchange for twenty-one burgenses. If the Castle, which still in part remains, was the one alluded to, it must have been built within the half century immediately preceding the Conquest, during which period Norman influence was manifest in English architecture. There is no earlier mention of a castle at Canterbury than that in Domesday, and although it has been supposed that the present building replaced an older castle there seems to be no evidence of it whatever. The castle is Norman in style, and very similar in general plan to

Rochester and other castles erected by the Conqueror. There only now remains the central keep which is remarkable for its area and massiveness. The walls, which are of enormous thickness, are composed of rubble; the round headed windows of the grand stage, the loops of the lower stages and the quoins of the walls were faced with ashlar stones. The surrounding court and ditch have long disappeared, and the keep, now a mere shell, has been turned into a coal store for the Gas Company. The history of the castle has not been remarkably eventful. It was used as a common prison as early as the time of Edward II., for in the Crown-rolls of that reign is a record that two prisoners, who sat chained to beg their bread at the barbican of the castle, escaped; the one took sanctuary in St. Mary de Castro, and the other, involuntarily drawn away by his companion, returned to his prison. During the periodical persecutions of the Jews in the middle ages many of that nation were imprisoned in the castle; it is recorded that centuries afterwards the walls remained inscribed with verses of the Psalms which they had carved in Hebrew characters on the stones.

Canterbury was surrounded by a wall of defence at a very early date. It is mentioned in one of the Ethelbertine charters of St. Augustine's, which is evidence at least of the supposed antiquity of the wall at the time that those fictitious charters were concocted. Roger of Hoveden, describing the siege of Canterbury by the Danes in 1011, says that many of the unfortunate citizens were cast headlong from the wall of the city. William of Malmesbury, writing in the reign of Stephen, speaks of Canterbury as being much renowned for the walls whole and undecayed enclosing it round about. It is not improbable that it was surrounded by a rampart of some kind as early as the period of the Roman occupation, although it is extremely doubtful if there was, as Mr. Godfrey Faussett argues in "Canterbury Till Domesday," a Roman wall around the city. The conical mound of the Dane John (as well as the lesser mounds which were formerly around it) might have been an early British work, which was afterwards included in the ramparts of a later period. The strengthening of the embankment with a casing of flint, the building of the towers, and the completion of the circuit of

THE WESTGATE TOWERS.

walls were carried out at various times subsequent to the conquest. In the reign of Richard I. vassals of the Prior of Christ Church were impressed to labour with other citizens at the fortification of the city with "ditches, walls and other fortresses." By the time of Richard II. the wall had ceased to be effective for defence, and was spoken of as tottering and decayed. The king gave a grant towards its repair, and at the same period Archbishop Sudbury built Westgate, and either erected or rebuilt part of the wall to Northgate. At the beginning of the next reign, however, the citizens were again labouring at the fortifications of the city, for a Royal writ of Henry IV., in the year 1403, says "Our well beloved, the citizens of our city of Canterbury, as we hear, have begun to fortify and strengthen the same city as well with one wall of stone as with a ditch." A survey of the city wall, taken in the previous year by Alderman Thomas Ickham, showed the whole circuit of the walls, with the seven gates and river to be 582½ perches.

The most ancient portion of the wall was undoubtedly that on the southern side of the city. Commencing at the right bank of the river, behind St. Mildred's Church it continued to the *Worthgate*, the site of which was probably in Castle Street, adjacent to the castle. Thence it bounded the Dane John, as it does at present, to the *Riding Gate*. From the Riding Gate we trace it, in what is now St. George's Terrace, to *St. George's Gate or Newingate*, which was the eastern part of the city; thence to *Burgate* (the present St. George's Lane is built upon the wall, and the houses on the west side of Bridge Street were built in the ditch). From Burgate it skirted Christ Church precincts to *Queeningate*, a small gate nearly opposite the grand gate of St. Augustine's Abbey; thence it continued to *Northgate*, from Northgate round to *Westgate*, and thence to the end of the circuit on the right bank of the river opposite St. Mildred's. It will be seen that anciently the city had seven gates, of which, thanks to the barbarism of the civic authorities in the early part of the present century, but one remains. Even that, the noble Westgate, was only spared from destruction, it is said, by the casting vote of the Mayor. There was also a gate called Wincheap Gate, but this formed no part of the ancient line of the city fortifications. It was rebuilt during the last century by a Dr. Jacob. Besides the seven gates there were a number of posterns or small gates for more convenient ingress or egress. When the walls were complete they were furnished with twenty-one watch towers, of which several still remain. On the Dane John there are four, all round; in the wall bounding the Cathedral precincts, the towers are remarkably interesting. In the Deanery garden the walk along the ramparts is still preserved, and the wall appears to be from six to seven feet thick. Numerous Roman tiles have been built into it, as well as a great many English bricks of a period previous to the taxing. The Deanery wall contains two square towers; the one nearest to Northgate is a mere ruin; the other is in a much better state of preservation, and below it is an arched cave or magazine. The square tower in Queeningate-lane, close to the Postern gate opposite St. Augustine's, was evidently an important position. It has a side cell with a look-out towards Northgate, and the remains of a fire-grate and chimney. The next is a round tower in the part of the wall, bounding the old Bowling-green. The whole internal surface of it has been honeycombed with some hundreds of cells, and doubtless it was the columbarium or dovecote of the monastery. There is a further round tower in the next garden of the Precincts. Between Northgate and Westgate some towers have been utilized as dwelling houses, and one has also been included in the mansion beyond Westgate, known as Tower House. The towers were arranged at such distances around the walls that a cross fire could be directed from the turret loops upon an enemy crossing the moat or attempting to scale the walls. A great part of the moat has been filled up, built upon, or converted into garden ground, but there is little difficulty in tracing it over a considerable distance.

The ancient Worthgate, of which a picture and description were given by Dr. Stukeley, was destroyed in 1791. It appears to have been a semi-circular arch of tiles, resting on piers of massive stones, the walls on either side showing several courses of tiles. Dr. Stukeley speaks of the arch as of Roman or British construction, and Somner describes it as "a perfect arch of British brick, not sampled of any

THE CASTLE, CITY WALLS, AND GATES.

other about the city." There has been a disposition to dispute that the Worthgate had the remote origin which these observations and the drawing of Dr. Stukeley would imply; there is little doubt, however, that the arch was round, was built of Roman tiles, and rested on piers of such large oolitic blocks as the Romans made use of in their buildings in Kent. (See p. 66). This must be regarded as strong evidence of the arch being as old as the Romano-British period.

Next to Worthgate was the Riding Gate, Radingate, or Roadgate, through which passed the ancient Watling Street, one of the four great ways crossing the country since the earliest times of British history. The Riding Gate also appears to have had vestiges of Roman arches. Somner speaks of Roman bricks still to be seen about it in his time, and Dr. Stukeley has given a drawing of the gate which shows parts of what were clearly round arches of tiles. One of the wall turrets stood by the side of the arch. Close to this gate there once stood the church of St. Edmund, King and Martyr; this Norman church was united to St. Mary Bredin's in 1349. It had formerly belonged to the Prioress and nuns of St. Sepulchre's, under grant from the Abbot of St. Augustine's. Every trace of the church has disappeared for centuries, but some skeletons were dug up on its site when excavations were made for the drainage works about fifteen years ago. The present Riding Gate was erected in 1791.

St. George's Gate, Newingate, or Newgate was standing until 1801, when the city authorities most needlessly went to great expense to destroy what they ought to have been proud to preserve. The date of its erection is not known, but it bore a marked resemblance to Westgate, like which it had round towers, a portcullis, and machiolated apertures above the drawbridge-port. It was probably erected about 1470, at which date a certain Wm. Bigg bequeathed ten pounds to "the making and performing of St. George's Gate." There had been a gate at that place before the end of the twelfth century however, for Newingate is named in a Bull of Alexander III. to the monks of Christ Church. We have heard from an old citizen a curious story in explanation of the destruction of St. George's Gate. It seems that it was customary for the

CANTERBURY CASTLE.

Commandant of the Garrison to place sentries at this gate, and frequent complaints had been made of the rudeness of the men, especially to ladies passing through the gate. The Mayor waited on the Commandant and asked him to take away the sentries. He replied that he could not remove them. "Then," said the Mayor, "we can remove the gate." Forthwith a Burghmote was called, and the order was given for the removal of the old structure. Such is the tale as we heard it some years ago from one who was old enough to have remembered the act of Vandalism.

Burgate or Borough Gate, sometimes called St. Michael's Gate, stood in the street which now retains its name. There was certainly a gate here in very early times, but the building, which was finally destroyed in 1822, was erected about 1475, as an inscription upon it recorded. Through this gate lay the high road to Sandwich, which was no doubt originally continued in a straight line to St. Martin's Hill, but was subsequently diverted into Longport by the monks of St. Augustine's, in order to enlarge the boundary of their cemetery. The right of way through the cemetery gate to St. Martin's was, according to Somner, the subject of a fierce dispute early in the reign of Henry VI. between the city bailiffs and the monks. The latter resisted the bailiffs in spite of their having the civic maces carried before them. The citizens got the better of the encounter, and then the monks went to law in the matter. Burgate, according to an old engraving of it, appears to have been flanked by octagonal towers.

"Come we now to Queeningate," says Somner, "but where shall we seek it? There is none of the name at this day; and few know where it stood. I sought as narrowly for it as for ants-paths, and at length having found it will show you where it was." The spot was a little beyond the postern gate still remaining, opposite St. Augustine's. Somner says a remnant of an arch of British bricks marked the site. Scattered Roman bricks are to be seen in abundance hereabout in the wall, but neither within nor without can any arch such as that spoken of be found. The wall in Queeningate-lane, close to the Deanery garden, shows a break in the ancient wall which has been filled up in recent times, and which is not unlikely to have been the spot alluded to by Somner. The Dean having kindly given us free access to the wall and ramparts, we sought narrowly for a clue to the site of the gate, but can only echo the old Rambler's question—"where shall we seek it?" The name Queeningate or Queen's Gate is suggestive of Queen Bertha, and has usually been ascribed to her. *If* the city was walled in the sixth century, and Ethelbert's palace was on the site of the Cathedral, and not on that of St. Augustine's, we can imagine Bertha using this gate on her way to St. Martin's. But the probabilities are greatly against the surmises. Somewhere near this gate formerly stood a church of St. Mary Queeningate.

Northgate stood under the church of St. Mary Northgate, and was destroyed when the old church was rebuilt.

Westgate, which alone remains to us of the city's seven gates, was erected in the reign of Richard II. by Archbishop Simon of Sudbury, who was murdered by Wat Tyler's men. Leland, in his quaint description of 'Cantorbyri,' says—"Sudbury builded the Westgate and made new and repaired to gither fro thens to the north gate, and wolde have done lykewise about al the town yf he had lyved. The mayr of the town and aldermen, ons a yere, cum solemply to his tumbe to pray for his sowle, yn memory of his good deade." This gate replaced an older one which had fallen into decay, and upon which stood Holy Cross Church. Westgate is a splendid example of a fortified city gate. On the east or inner side a large square tower stands over a fine pointed archway, the roof of which is vaulted; on the west side the square central building is flanked by two circular towers, one on either side of the gate, which was defended by a portcullis, and by the machiolated apertures through which boiling water, molten metal, and other means of a warm reception, could be showered on an enemy who had gained possession of the drawbridge, or crossed the river which was then open to the towers. The holes may still be seen through which the chains of the bridge passed; the grooves of the portcullis also remain. The towers on the outer side have no windows, but numerous loops through which the enemy could be aimed at. On the city side the great room which is over the archway has a fine pointed window which commands a view of the main streets. In the opposite wall is a recess, apparently for the portcullis when raised. From this room access is obtained to the circular towers with their gloomy cells. Some of these are lighted only by loops, trebly barred with iron gratings. The cells which open to the roof have strong iron-grated doors through which the prisoners could be seen by a warder on the outside. For several centuries this old tower was used as the city prison, and here all kinds of prisoners appear to have been cast indiscriminately. The place, within the memory of persons still living, was a foul and horrible den, in which the unfortunate debtor shared alike with the felon the filth and horrors of the prison. The felons, however, were heavily manacled, and in one of the cells we found but the other day quite a collection of their leg chains—ponderous iron links, some of them weighing at least thirty dounds. A strong iron ring in the floor of one of the towers was used no doubt to chain up a refractory or desperate criminal. We could but remember as we lingered in the dismal cells that among the prisoners who have been enjailed and tortured, there were many poor men and women whose only crime was loyalty to their God; martyrs whose faith enabled them to endure not only the cruelties of their prison, but the subsequent death at the stake. In the brief but horrible epoch of the Marian persecution, not less than forty-one men and women were burnt to death in the martyr's field near Wincheap.

CHAPTER XVII.

Priories, Nunneries, and Alms Houses in Canterbury.

HE Black Friars or Dominicans were seen for the first time in Canterbury in 1221; the first Grey Friars or Franciscans arrived in 1224; and the White Friars or Augustine Friars took up their abode here about a century later. The rival orders soon established themselves in the city, and were active agents in the religious life of the middle ages, but only a few remains of their extensive monastic buildings are left in our day. The Dominicans or Preaching Friars appear to have been first welcomed to Canterbury by Archbishop Stephen Langton, but it was not till the year 1236 that they returned to settle in the city. This was in the part of St. Alphege parish which still retains the name of Blackfriars. The chief of the three entrances to the monastery was by a gateway in St. Peter's Street, nearly opposite Eastbridge Hospital. It was built in the time of Edward III., and was of squared flints, with a pointed arch, niches, and other ornaments. It was pulled down towards the end of the last century. The church of the monastery has entirely disappeared, but the Unitarian Chapel in the Black Friars is part of the ancient refectory. It has been much altered, but contains some of the original pointed windows, each of two-lights, with quatrefoil head. A door in the gallery opens into a small square tower; this contains a pointed arch which appears to have led to a staircase. On the opposite side of the river, upon the island of Binnewith, were some further buildings and grounds belonging to the monastery. The

THE GREY FRIARS.

extent of the enclosed land was rather more than five acres. The chief royal patron of the preaching friars was Henry I., who not only granted them land for their buildings, but mainly provided the funds for the erection of their church. He also gave them a great part of the oak timber required, while the Archbishop gave them allowance of firewood. The position of the several buildings of the Priory is known from an old drawing and plan of them made soon after the Dissolution. From the St. Peter's gate a long road called the "Friars' Way" passed to the river, which it crossed on a bridge of three pointed arches, and on the opposite bank fell into another way leading from the St. Alphege gate to the main group of buildings. These formed a Quadrangle, enclosing the friars' cloisters; the church was on the south side of it, the churchyard being south of that; the refectory, dormitories, kitchen and other offices completed the Quadrangle. Within the Priory there was anciently a Guild or Fraternity of the Parish Clerks of the city, called the Brotherhood of St. Nicholas. The Priory fell with other monastic houses in 1538, but three years earlier the Prior had been cited to appear in Archbishop Cranmer's court. Cranmer had been preaching in the Cathedral against the authority and supremacy of the Pope, and the Prior had dared to publicly maintain the Pope's cause against the Archbishop, whereby Cranmer, writing to the king, declared himself to be "m'velously sclawndered in thies parties." The Priory became private property, and passed from one to another until in 1658 it was purchased by one Peter de la Pierre, a surgeon from Flanders, who introduced the Anabaptists here. The sect established their meeting house in the old refectory, and used a part of the Friars' cemetery as their burial ground. The churchyard still contains some old memorials of the Baptists of the last century, including one to a Mrs. "Experience" Brown. Somner mentions that the churchyard was in 1640 "the Artillery Ground for the young artillery of the city." In the time of Edward I. it appears to have been the rendezvous of the citizens in a plot they entered into against the monks of Christ Church, who had refused to share in furnishing twelve horsemen demanded by the King. The citizens engaged in an early case of boycotting. They forbade any man to "send or sell to the monks any victuals," or to pay rent for any house belonging to them; they threatened to stop all men from going into or coming out of the monastery, and "to spoil of their garments any monks who ventured forth;" but the fractious citizens were appeased by the Archbishop.

The Grey Friars first came to Canterbury in 1224. They were a company of four clerics and five laymen, and were lodged their first night in a small-room under the school-house of Christ Church, where, in the evening, some of the scholars joined them, and "all made merry, drinking from one pot." The new comers were next taken in by the Provost of the Poor Priests' Hospital, who gave them "a plot of ground set out with a convenient house and a decent chapel or oratory." In 1270 Alderman John Diggs, an ancestor of Sir Dudley Digges, of Chilham Castle, bought and presented to them the island of Binnewith, formed by the divided branches of the Stour. Here they established their monastery, which had one entrance in Stour Street, and another in St. Peter's, the latter by a gateway which stood over against that of the rival order of Dominicans. The Franciscans in Canterbury certainly did not observe their rule of poverty, but soon became possessed of goodly property. They lost no opportunity of enriching themselves by granting sepulture in their church to wealthy citizens as a reward for benefactions to their monastery. They had not long been settled in Binnewith before they began to seize on houses and lands belonging to Christ Church, and in the disputes which arose out of this, the Friars, who had vowed to possess no property whatever, held so firmly to their ill-gotten estate that they ultimately secured it at about half its rental. Of the buildings of the monastery there remains a very curious and interesting old house, built on pointed arches over the river. There are also a few portions of the old boundary walls still to be seen in the surrounding gardens. This old house of the Grey Friars was for some time the residence of members of the Lovelace family. Wm. Lovelace, serjeant-at-law, was counsel for the city of Canterbury during a portion of the reign of Queen Elizabeth, and also sat for the city in Parliament.

He died, in 1677, in some remarkable way, the history of which is now unknown, but it was the subject of various publications at the time. He was buried in the Cathedral. He not only owned the Grey Friars, but had bought the St. Lawrence estate, a purchase which involved him in a costly law suit. His son seems to have suffered from the ungenerous ill will of Sir Roger Manwood, the Chief Baron of the Exchequer, between whom and the elder Lovelace there had been enmity. This son, who was knighted in 1599, unsuccessfully contested Canterbury in 1624. Five years later he died at the old house of the Grey Friars. His grandson was the celebrated Cavalier, Richard Lovelace, who was declared to be "the most amiable and beautiful person that eye ever beheld." He was the most handsome man at the Court of Charles I., and was a soldier, dramatist, and poet. He played a prominent part in the great Rebellion, and was chosen at Maidstone to deliver the famous Kentish Petition in 1642, for "the restoration of the King to his rights," a petition which was burned by the common hangman. It was during his imprisonment for his part in this transaction that he is said to have written the lines:—

> " Stone walls do not a prison make
> Nor iron bars a cage ;
> Mindes innocent and quiet take
> That for an hermitage ;
> If I have freedom in my love,
> And in my soule am free,
> Angels alone that soare above
> Enjoy such liberty."

The closing days of his life were in striking contrast to the brilliant promise and favour of his early manhood. He is described as having become melancholy, poor, ragged, an object of charity ; living in obscure and wretched abodes. He died in London at the age of forty, in a miserable lodging in Gunpowder Alley, Shoe Lane.

The White or Augustine Friars first came to Canterbury in the year 1325, and having established themselves in a house in St. George's parish, built a chapel, and began to celebrate mass. This was regarded as poaching on the preserves of the parish priest, and the Archbishop gave orders for an interdict to issue against the newly-arrived mendicants. The affair was settled by a compromise, the Friars agreeing to pay the parson of St. George's nine shillings yearly. Of the Priory of White Friars scarcely a trace now remains. The principal entrance was by a gateway in St. George's Street. The Middle Schools now occupy the site of the ancient buildings.

The suppression of these three orders in Canterbury was carried out by Ingworth, Bishop Suffragan of Dover, on December 14th, 1538, as appears from a letter of his to Lord Cromwell, reporting his progress in the affair:—" The xiij day of dece'ber I cam to ca't'bury wher y^t I fynde iij howseys, more in dett than all y^t they have ys abull to pay, & specyally ye austen fryers . . . . ye blacke and gray be abull w^t ther impleme'ts to pay ther detts and for ow^r costs, and lytyll more . . . . & so this sonday I woll make an ende in ca't'bury, and on mu'day to sandwyche."

The Priory of St. Gregory in Northgate Street has already been spoken of in connection with St. John's Hospital. It was originally founded by Lanfranc for secular priests, but it was changed in the time of Henry I. into a Priory of regular Canons. A small part of the ruined buildings remained at the close of the last century, but now not a trace of them can be seen.

The Poor Priests' Hospital, to which reference has been made, was founded by Archdeacon Simon Langton, in or about 1240. Thorn says that he founded it with the charity of others. Its name sufficiently explains its purpose. The livings of Stodmarsh and St. Margaret's, Canterbury, were granted to the Hospital within a few years of its foundation. The Poor Priests were spared at the Dissolution of the Monasteries, but in 1575 the Hospital and its estates were transferred to the Mayor and citizens of Canterbury. Its use then became twofold— a hospital school for poor children, and a bridewell or House of Correction. In 1728 it became the Workhouse, the property being passed over to the Guardians of the Poor, who were to clothe, feed, and educate sixteen poor boys, and to hand the surplus of the estate to the city authorities to lessen the poor rates. A few years ago a scheme was passed by which the estates were transferred to the Governors of the Middle Schools, who are at present the administrators of the largely increased income of the ancient charity. The buildings ceased to be used as a workhouse when the present Union-house was erected. Some portions of the old Hospital remain; not of the earliest building, however, as it was "new-built of stone" in 1733.

The Hospital of St. Lawrence, the name of which survives in the adjacent County Cricket Ground, was founded in 1137 by the Abbot of St. Augustine, as a lazar-house for leprous monks and sisters. In the time of Edward III. it ceased to be used for brothers; in the reign of Henry VIII. the Hospital was leased to Sir Christopher Hales, free of rent for nine years, on condition of providing for the prioress and sisters during their lives. By 1562 the number had dwindled down to two. The estate subsequently became the seat of Sir George Rooke (see p. 77). It afterwards passed to Viscount Dudley and Ward, and at the present time it belongs to Earl Sondes. There was formerly on one of the piers of the old gateway a figure of St. Lawrence on the gridiron, with a man standing at his head and another at his feet. The sculptured stone still remains in the old wall, but the figures upon it are almost wholly obscured.

Somewhat nearer to the city than the Hospital of St. Lawrence was the Nunnery of St. Sepulchre's of which but a small piece of wall remains in the grounds of the Hoystings. It was a Benedictine nunnery founded by Anselm in 1100, and is memorable in history as the abode of the so called Holy Maid of Kent, Elizabeth Barton. The story of this famous nun of St. Sepulchre's has been fully and graphically told by Mr. Froude. Elizabeth Barton was an instrument in the hands of those who regarded the divorce of Henry from Catherine of Aragon with horror, and who still more disliked the severance of the English church from Rome. The poor girl was one of those hysterical subjects who are likely to fall into trances, and to see visions. She was quickly tutored by the arts of those around her, and her ravings were declared to be revelations of the Divine will. Her fame was spread abroad, and many great people had interviews with the nun-prophetess. Archbishop

PRIORIES AND NUNNERIES.

Warham introduced her by letter to Wolsey as "a very well disposed and vertuouse woman as I am enformed by her susters." Sir Thomas More saw and conversed with her. Her visions, unhappily for her, were directed into the channel of treason; she denounced the king's divorce, and predicted his speedy death. Henry was not of the metal to be bent by such means; but the poor tool was broken. The nun and a number of her confederates were tried in the Star Chamber. She and several others, including the Warden of the Grey Friars, and the cellarer of Christ Church, were executed in April, 1534. Fisher, Bishop of Rochester, and Sir Thomas More narrowly escaped then, but their fate was only postponed till the summer of the following year, when both were beheaded.

The ground upon which the modern houses stand, on the side of the old Dover Road opposite to the Hoystings, appears to have been the cemetery of the nunnery, in which it seems probable that interments were granted to others than the nuns of St. Sepulchre's. In the opening up of the ground for the foundations of the new houses, skeletons were found at a depth of about four feet, so thick together that Mr. Brent describes them as lying shoulder to shoulder, presenting a ghastly spectacle. These remains showed no trace of coffins, and we believe the general impression at the time was that the densely crowded collection of human remains indicated the hurried interment of a large number of victims at some visitation of the plague. About two feet below this layer of skeletons the excavators came upon a more ancient cemetery, evidently Roman. It contained a great number of sepulchral urns, and such objects as are usually found associated with them in Roman burial places. Below this second deposit of human remains there were evidences of a third still more ancient, the human bones unburnt, the interments apparently belonging to the Celtic period. It is remarkable that this spot at St. Sepulchre's should thus be stratified with the dead of three several races.

At the farther end of Wincheap stood the Hospital of St. James, or as it is more generally known St. Jacob's (Jacobus), founded during the twelfth century for twenty-five leprous sisters, a prioress, and attendant priests. It escaped the general fate of such establishments at the Dissolution, but only to fall, very shortly after, into the hands of persons who seized and divided the property. In 1557 there was but one sister still alive.

Besides these ancient religious houses brief mention must be made of a number of charitable foundations of later date. In Northgate is Jesus Hospital, founded as an alms-house for eight poor men and four women by Sir John Boys, the first Recorder of Canterbury, who died in 1612. Cogan's Hospital, founded in 1657, in St. Peter's Street, as an alms-house for poor widows of clergymen, has of late years been removed to new buildings in the London Road. Maynard's or Cotton's Hospital is in St. Mildred's. The first founder was John Maynard, called the Rich, who in 1312 left estates for the maintenance of four brothers and three sisters. In 1604 Alderman Cotton left property to maintain an additional brother and two sisters. The deeds of the Hospital were destroyed in the Great Fire of London, 1666. There are some other alms-houses in the city which do not fall within the scope of the present work.

CHAPTER XVIII.

Thanington and Tonford.

Corbel, Tonford.

FEW, perhaps, who visit Thanington are aware that it is one of the country churchyards for which the honor has been claimed of being the churchyard of the Elegy. Many years ago this claim was ably set forth in the columns of the *Athenæum* by the Rev. William Pearson, then vicar of the church. Whether Gray did actually derive inspiration for his matchless elegy in the little churchyard of Thanington we cannot say, but he must have been familiar with the spot when resident at Canterbury. It was then much more secluded than at present, the road which now passes it having been made during the present century. It might certainly have suggested not a few of the pictures in Gray's exquisite verses. We can imagine the poet walking out across the meadows to Thanington and resting for quiet meditation beneath its venerable "yew-tree's shade," in view of those grand Cathedral towers beyond, whence still "The curfew tolls the knell of parting day."

The church, dedicated to St. Nicholas, is mainly Early English, but a portion of the walls is of Norman masonry, and the chancel has two small round-headed Norman windows, The east window is a double lancet. The church is now undergoing restoration, and the architect, Mr. John Cowell, is carrying out the work with praiseworthy care to preserve the ancient character of the building. The present plan of the church consists of a nave and chancel which are continuous, a south chancel, opening without arches to the nave, its roof most inadequately supported by timber uprights. The cruciform plan is completed by a north tower, opening to the nave by a pointed arch. The works now in progress include the erection of a chancel arch and an arcade of two arches to the south chapel. This chapel will be greatly improved by the removal of an utterly incongruous square window inserted in a previous restoration; two lancet windows will be substituted. The nave at present has but a single pointed window on the south side and a late pointed two-light west window. The north wall is being pierced for two additional windows. These and the additions throughout will be in Early English style, to harmonize with the general character of the ancient building. An interesting discovery has been made that there was originally a south aisle with two Early English arches. When these were filled in a window was inserted in one arch, and the present south door in the other. The original door was at the west end. The existence of this aisle was wholly unsuspected. The tower was erected within the present century to replace the old one which had fallen. Hasted speaks of several inscribed tombstones in the chancel, but only a single one remains; it has a very perfect brass, the armoured figure being that of Thomas Halle, Esquire, 1485. The stolen brasses included two to the memory of Sir Charles Hales (1623) and his lady, Anne (1617). In the south wall of the chancel is what Hasted terms a tomb, but it has more the appearance of one of those ancient confessionals in which the priest sat within, while the penitent knelt outside the church, so that he might be shriven without being seen. The east windows were filled with painted glass by the late Miss Hetty Betty Sankey, and some other windows by Mrs. Powell, of St. Dunstan's. The only bit of old glass remaining is in the east window of the chapel—a head of Our Lord. The churchyard contains a fine old yew, probably as old as the church. The lych gate was erected as a memorial of the Rev. William Pearson, for many years vicar of the parish. There is a curious circumstance connected with the vicarage of Thanington. It anciently consisted of two rooms under the roof of the old Cockering Farm-house, the quaint old place still standing on the upper road to Ashford. A large field adjoining it is known as the vicarage field, but when this and the modest vicarage were alienated from the living we have failed to discover. The living of Thanington at one time

Thanington Church.

pertained to St. Gregory's Priory. The Registers are in complete and excellent preservation, dating from the "ye begininge of ye Queene's Maiestie's raigne, viz., ye 17 daye of Nov., 1558."

The ford beside Thanington and the road which leads to it, carry us back two thousand years, to the time when these were the way between the two British camps or towns at Iffin and Bigbury. Each of these camps will well repay a visit; for, although overgrown with wood, there is not the slightest difficulty in making out the ancient mounds, ramparts, and trenches. The most remarkable feature at Iffin is a tumulus, 150 feet in circumference and nearly six feet high; it stands a little distance west of the entrenchments. This tumulus was opened some years ago by Mr. Bell, of Bourne Park, and five urns were discovered in it. They were rudely formed of half-baked clay, containing particles of flint; but one was of a very unusual size for urns of the Celtic age, its height being 25 inches, its diameter 22 inches. The urns contained ashes and fragments of bones; they were all found with the mouths downwards, and were closed with clay. The tumulus is formed of brick earth, almost entirely free from pebbles. The camp at Bigbury and Howfield woods lies just behind Tonford, its length being, in the direction from east to west, about three furlongs; its breadth, from north to south, two furlongs. A double bank with trench forms the outer line of defence, a single bank and trench the inner line. The shape is irregular, and evidently resulted from the natural formation of the ground.

Thanington and Toniford manors are not mentioned in the Domesday survey; in the time of the Conqueror the former, under the name of Tenitune, is mentioned as included in the Archbishop's manor of Westgate. It was early held by the Valoyns family, and in the reign of Edward III. by Sir William de Septvans; in the time of Richard II. it belonged to Sir William Waleys; in that of Richard III. to the above-mentioned Thomas Halle; from the reign of Henry VIII. to that of Elizabeth it was the residence of the Hales family. The manor of Toniford, Tonford, or Tunford stood on the north bank of the river opposite Thanington. In the reign of Henry III. it was the residence of John de Toniford; it subsequently became the seat of the Fogges, and by the reign of Henry VI. had passed to Sir Thomas Browne, to whom the right was granted to "embattle and impark within his manor of Tonford."

The melancholy fate of Sir James Hales attaches a sombre interest to Thanington and Tonford. He was the eldest son of Sir John Hales, of the Dungeon, and was a Justice of the Common Pleas at the time when the dying young king, Henry VI., had been induced to set aside his sister Mary, and name Lady Jane Grey as his successor. Nine Judges signed a deed of assent to this; but Sir James Hales,

though an earnest Protestant, refused to do so, declaring it to be
unjust and unlawful. When Mary had established herself on the throne,
the loyalty of the upright judge did not save him. He was disgraced,
dismissed, imprisoned, and persecuted until he yielded to the pressure,
and recanted. He went down to his nephew's house at Thanington
crushed in mind by remorse at his weakness. " Melancholy marked him
for her own," and shortly after he was drowned in the Stour at Tonford.
Harris says he probably fell in, being aged and weak; other historians
accept the recorded verdict of *felo de se*, as a proof that he committed
suicide. It is supposed that the curious pleadings offered in a lawsuit
arising out of this verdict, suggested to Shakespeare the argument of the
gravediggers in *Hamlet* :—

1 *Clown*. Here lies the water; good : here stands the man ; good : If the man
go to this water, and drown himself, it is, will he, nil he, he goes ; mark you that :
But if the water come to him, and drown him, he drowns not himself: Argal, he that
is not guilty of his own death, shortens not his own life.

2 *Clown*. But is this law ?

1 *Clown*. Ay, marry is 't ; crowner's-quest law.

In tracing out the connection of the Hales family with Thanington,
we were led to examine the curious monument of another Sir James
Hales in the nave of Canterbury Cathedral. This Sir James died and
was buried at sea, on his return from a Portuguese expedition, and in
his monument he is represented being dropped into the sea. Almost
hidden behind the kneeling figure of his lady, there is a marble slab on
which there is a very old painting of a landscape. We made a close
inspection of this picture, and found it to be a representation of Thanington Church ; while, across the river, and in the background, there is a
castellated edifice with lofty walls and round towers—the ancient Toniford
manor undoubtedly. Why should this view of Thanington have been
painted on the monument of Sir James Hales ? In the picture there are
four men, with poles in their hands, apparently hastening to the river.
Are the sculptures and the painting meant to be memorials of two family
disasters—Sir James drowned at Tonford in 1555, and another Sir
James buried at sea in 1589 ? It is interesting, in any case, to have a

REMAINS OF TONFORD MANOR.

16th century picture of the manor. The remains at Tonford confirm the general accuracy of the view. On the north side of the present farmhouse are two round towers at the angles, similar in character to those of the painting. That these are remains of the ancient building we cannot doubt, and indeed this part of the house contains more extensive relics of the castellated mansion than is generally known.

By the courtesy of Mr. Bing, the tenant, we have been able to go into all parts of the building, and to explore it thoroughly, the result being singularly interesting. The doorway shown in the accompanying sketch (p. 118) opens to the ancient kitchen, a spacious apartment lighted by a fine three-light window. The great fireplace is evidently as old as the Tudor building, and so also is the apartment adjoining. We were wholly unprepared, however, to find the ancient roof still preserved. In the range of bed-rooms, our attention was directed to some pendant-posts, which, though covered by papering, and partly hidden in the ceiling, evidently belonged to a timber roof. Mr. Bing kindly permitted us to get into the gabled roof through a small aperture, and, lights having been passed in, there was at once revealed a very handsome timber roof, the wood, oak or chestnut, so remarkably preserved that it might have dated from a few years instead of centuries. The rafters and cross-bars of the panelling are moulded or chamfered, and the collar-braces form three elegant pointed arches, with moulded edges. We should imagine this fine open roof, which extends the whole length of the building, to have belonged to the chapel of the manor. It is singular that, hidden away so long in the dark roof of the old farm-house, this most interesting and perfect relic of old Tonford manor should have remained unnoticed; we have sought in vain the slightest allusion to it. In one of the external walls beyond the house, are two corbels and niches, which might also have belonged to the chapel. They are nearly alike, the brackets being supported by winged female figures, bearing shields. The figures have curiously-waved hair, and wear collars of ecclesiastical cut. There is a very similar corbel in Boughton Aluph Church. The carving is very delicate, and, in spite of long exposure to the weather, well preserved.

TUDOR GATEWAY, TONFORD.

The wing-marking is remarkably clear. The wall in which these corbels have been inserted, contains a round tower, not shown in the sketch of the main building; it has a very small pointed window. At the foot of this wall and all round the circuit of the house was a moat, which was only filled up a generation back. The drawbridge was in use until the moat was done away with; it was at the fine Tudor gate, of which a sketch is given. It will be admitted, we think, that Tonford is a place of remarkable interest; we are glad to add that the present tenant appreciates its value as an ancient relic, and is careful to preserve it from injury.

There is one further point of interest to mention in relation to Thanington. Opposite the church is a large field long known as Up-and-Down Field. Mr. J. M. Cowper maintains that this is Chaucer's "Bob-up-and-down," of the Manciple's Tale. It is usually supposed that Chaucer meant Harbledown, but there has always been some doubt about it, and Mr. Cowper argues very ably against the accepted theory. (See *The Athenæum*, Dec. 26, 1868, and Mr. Furnivall's "Temporary Preface to Chaucer's Canterbury Tales," published for the Chaucer Society).

CHAPTER XIX.

Milton, Horton, and Chartham.

ITHERTO our rambles have been within the city, or to the parishes next beyond it. In the following pages we propose to describe much more briefly the points of interest in the villages immediately encircling Canterbury. In a walk to Chartham, the upper road (which is the ancient way) affords the most charming views of the Stour valley, with its characteristic Kentish landscape. As we ascend the hill from Wincheap, we see below us the charming little church of Thanington, the old ford, and the ruined walls of Tonford manor; while over marsh and lea the eye ranges to Bigbury with its British camp, to Harbledown on the crest of the hill, and old St. Nicholas' Hospital on the slope below it; to the city with the Cathedral towering above it, or still farther to the pale outline of the distant Thanet shore. We cross the old British path from Iffin to the ford, trodden by ancient Celts ages before Roman legions or Jutish immigrants came this way; and presently we come to old Cockering Farm, the nearest corner of which was once the vicarage of Thanington. Thence, passing Cockering Wood with its primrose glades and nightingale groves, we arrive at Milton, one of the smallest of English parishes, for it has only two houses and less than a dozen parishioners. Milton manor was granted to Christ Church before the Conquest. In Domesday it is entered as held by Hamo de Crévequer. At a later date it belonged to the Septvans and other noble families. The tiny parish church is

prettily situated on the hillside: it is dedicated to St. Nicholas, like its neighbour Thanington, and Lanfranc's church at Harbledown. It consists of a nave and chancel, in the Early English style, but the present structure is mainly the work of the restorer.

Next we reach Chartham Downs, and pass the spot which "Master Tom Ingoldsby" has celebrated in his legend of "Nell Cook and the Dark Entry," as that whereon "Charles Storey, too, his friend who slew," was "gibbeted on Chartham Downs." (Bentley's edition says *Chatham*, a palpable misprint). We traced in the Register of Chartham the entry of the burial of Storey's friend, a papermaker at the mill:—"Henry Perkins, who was most inhumanly murdered by Charles Storey, was buried May 25th, 1782." Storey was hung on Oaten-hill, and was gibbeted in chains on "Chartham Downs." It was to his gibbet the Mayor of Canterbury alluded when, as Barham tells us, he begged Archbishop Moore to allow him to have the honour of attending his Grace *as far as the gallows.*"

On the south bank of the river below the Downs stands Horton Chapel, and the site of Horton manor. The manor was one of the estates granted by the Conqueror to his turbulent half-brother Odo. No remains of the manor are now to be seen, but considerable foundations are met with adjacent to the present buildings. The old chapel of the manor, which has given the farm its name, ceased to be used for religious purposes when the mansion fell into disrepair; it is at present used as a hop-oast.

Where the Kent County Asylum now stands on Chartham, or Kenville, Down, there was formerly a considerable Saxon cemetery. The numerous barrows, some eighty in all, were long supposed to be connected with Cæsar's advance into Britain, and to mark the site of a battle between the Romans and the Britons. The Rev. Bryan Faussett, in 1773, opened up the graves, and carefully described, in his "Inventorium Sepulchrale," the remains found in them. The graves were from two to six feet deep; the bodies had, in many cases, been buried in wooden coffins, which had been charred to make them more durable. The skeletons were those of men, women, and children; a very few darts and javelins were found, but many articles of ordinary use, knife-blades, buckles, pins, beads, and trinkets of various kinds. One of the objects was a cross of silver with a centre boss of silver in a socket of gold. This Christian emblem was on the neck of a female skeleton. The whole surface of the Chartham and neighbouring Downs formerly showed remains of trenches, embankments, and tumuli, but many have been levelled by the plough, or obscured by overgrowth of wood.

We descend the hill into Chartham, a village of respectable antiquity, and of considerable importance in early times. "Certeham" is named in Domesday as one of the pre-Norman manors belonging to Christ Church. It remained in the possession of that monastery until the Dissolution, and was a rural retreat for the Abbot. In it Archbishop Winchelsea found an asylum when, having fallen under the displeasure of Edward I., his estates were seized by the King.

On the dissolution of Christ Church monastery, the manor of Chartham was settled on the newly-established Dean and Chapter, and the mansion-house became a residence of the Deans of Canterbury. It was the favourite abode of Dean Bargrave, who was also rector of Chartham. A few remains of the ancient manor-house are included in the present "Chartham Deanery." The paper-mill at Chartham, though not the oldest in the county, has been long established. It was originally a fulling-mill, and was converted by Peter Archer (who died in 1737) into a paper-mill. There formerly stood by the village-green a large mansion, the residence of the Kingsford family; it was destroyed by fire, and was long known as the "Burnt House." There is still remaining, though much modernised, the house built by Dr. De L'Angle, a Canon of Canterbury, and Rector of Chartham, who died in 1729. In front of De L'Angle House is a fine marble bust of Charles II.

The Church, dedicated to St. Mary, is cruciform, the transepts being extremely shallow. There are no aisles; the west tower is bold and massive; the nave is plain but lofty; while the chancel is large and handsome. There is a good south porch with trefoiled windows and timber roof. The tower, which is 70 feet to the vane, is of much later date than the church; it has a square stair turret on the north. Like the rest of the structure, it is built of flint, the buttresses being chequered with squared stone. The tower was evidently a work of the Tudor period; the nave and transepts are probably due to the earliest portion of the Decorated period, the chancel being somewhat later work. The absence of aisles increases the effect of length and height. There is a lofty, unbroken Perpendicular tower-arch opening to the nave; the latter is sparsely lighted in comparison with the splendid chancel; its windows are short double lancets, trefoiled, under splayed arches. The piers at the junction of the nave and transepts are each pierced with a 'Squint,'

There is a very fine timber roof. The chancel is strikingly light and spacious; it has an east window of four lights, containing beautiful tracery. In each of the side walls there are four two-light windows, all with elegant star tracery; they have recently been filled with stained glass, but in some of them there still remain some relics of the beautiful original glass. The roof is panelled, the ribs having carved bosses. The hoods of the chancel windows are all connected by small trefoils. In the north wall is an arched tomb, said to contain a leaden coffin; the stonework is a restoration from the original pattern. The Chartham brasses have often been described and figured; the oldest and finest—that of Sir Robert de Septvans—is one of the earliest of the incised brasses still extant in this country; it is of special interest as the memorial of a notable member of that famous Kentish family. This Sir Robert was born in 1250, and served with Edward I. in Scotland, being knighted at the siege of Carlaveroch. He sat in Parliament as Knight of the Shire, his residence being at that manor of Milton, to which we have already alluded. The brass has the figure of a cross-legged knight, in coat of mail, the surcoat and ailettes, as well as the shield, bearing the heraldic winnowing fans of the Septvans. Sir Robert was buried in the chancel of Chartham Church in 1306, which there is good reason to think is about the date of the chancel, although it has usually been described as later.

The next oldest of the brasses bears the figure of a priest, wearing a cope: it is that of Robert London, 1416, a rector of Chartham. There are also brasses of two other rectors—Robert Arthur, 1454, and Robert

Sheffelde, 1508. There is besides these, a small brass bearing the figure of a lady, and this inscription—"Off your charyte pray for the soul of Jane Dowther of Lewys Clefforht, obt. 1530"—*i.e.* Jane, daughter of Lewis Clifford.

On the east wall of the chancel is a small monument, in the Elizabethan style, to the memory of "MR. JOHN BUNGEYE, CLERKE, ONE OF Y᷎ᴱ PREBENDARIES OF CHRIST CHURCH IN CANT., AND PARSON OF THIS PARISHE," * * * "WHICH JOHN BYLDED MYSTOLE, AND THERE DIED Y᷎ᴱ 20 NOVEB., A.O. 1596. Among other monuments is one by Rysbrach, to Sir Wm. and Lady Young, the latter a daughter of Charles Fagge, Esq., of Mystole.

The Registers of Chartham commence in 1558, but are not complete. We sought in vain for the autograph of "Blue Dick," as the notorious Richard Culmer was called. On the death of Dean Bargrave, in 1642, Culmer got himself appointed to the rectory of Chartham, Archbishop Laud being then in the Tower. He was the ringleader of the attacks upon the Cathedral, and the chief agent in smashing the painted glass of the beautiful window given by Edward IV. He himself describes the exploit thus :—"Whilst judgment was executing on the Idols in that window, the Cathedralists cryed out againe for their great Diana—'Hold your hands, holt, holt, heers Sir,' etc. A Minister being then on the top of the Citie ladder, neer 60 steps high, with a whole pike in his hand rattling down proud Becket's glassy bones (others then present would not adventer so high), to him it was said, ' 'Tis a shame for a Minister to be seen there.' The Minister replied, 'Sir, I count it no shame, but an honour. My Mʳ· whipt the living buyers and sellers out of the Temple; these are dead Idols, which defile the worship of God here, being the fruits and occasions of Idolatry.' Some wished it might breake his neck; others said it should cost bloud. But he finished the worke, and came downe well, and was in very good health when this was written."

Culmer was called "Blue Dick" from his habit of wearing blue instead of the clerical black. He was born in Thanet and was educated at Canterbury; he is said to have held the livings of Chartham,

Goodnestone, Harbledown, and St. Stephen's. He was buried at last at Monkton. His hold over Chartham was but short: we could find no trace of him in the Register, which is almost a blank during the period of the great Civil War. There are no entries at all from 1638 to 1645, and only twelve during the next four years. The Register contains numerous entries of money paid for killing foxes and "grays" (badgers). The price seems to have been a shilling a head.

On the upper road between Chartham and Chilham is Mystole Park and the mansion, which Parson John Bungeye 'bylded.' It is most pleasantly situated above the Stour valley, with Penny Pot Wood at its back. How long-lived are names! This "Penny Pot" is but the corruption of the Celtic name, Pen-y-pwth, the "crown of the hill." On Pen-y-pwth, the grave mounds of some of the British people who called it by that name are still to be seen.

Our way now leads us down the hill through the straggling hamlet of Shalmsford Street. Here at the bridge across the Stour below, there stood an important manor, owned at the time of the Conquest by a noble Saxon named Alret, who fought at Hastings. It was subsequently divided into two separate manors—Shalmsford Street and Shalmsford Bridge, the latter being the most important. In the reign of Edward II., the daughter and heiress of William de Shamelesford married one John Petit, and various members of the Petit family possessed the manor down to the end of James I.

CHAPTER XX.

HILHAM CASTLE is one of the least known of our ancient fortresses; it is rarely visited, and still less often described. Few appear to appreciate its singular interest and antiquity. By the kind permission of C. S. Hardy, Esq., we have been able to repeatedly visit and examine it. Hasted says the keep is plainly Norman; but it differs in several respects from the castles of Norman builders, and we have little doubt that part of the structure is much earlier than the Conquest. Its octagonal keep most closely resembles the simple tower-fortresses of an earlier and ruder age, the strongholds of petty kings or tribal chiefs. It is notable for its huge thickness of wall and small-contained area; the external diameter of the octagon is but 39 feet, while the walls have an irregular thickness of from 8 to 10 feet, leaving but a small clear space within. The extension of a square wing on one side of the octagon seems to have been made subsequent to the main tower. The court around the keep is of made ground, and is surrounded by a very high wall, except on the side on which the extended part coincides with the line of that wall. On this side the depth from the parapet of the keep to the present level of the ground is about 60 feet. Such a plan is quite unlike the regular Norman castle of the period to which this has been ascribed. The rude character of the masonry, the small dimensions of the apartments, the singular

height of the court, the disproportionate thickness of the walls all tend to confirm the old tradition that Chilham Castle was standing before the Normans entered the country. Traces of Caen stone, or Norman mouldings in the windows, are no proof of its being a Norman structure as a whole. The present entrances are manifestly not the original, but later piercings of the walls. The spiral staircase also is a recent renewal of the old one. The dungeon below the keep had been filled up for centuries, but a few years ago Mr. Hardy had it excavated. Its shape is the same as the keep; its walls are of enormous thickness, and are pierced by three slants, originally with very small loops in the outer walls. Mr. Hardy caused a tunnel to be driven under the castle, commencing in the slope of the mound below the north west wall of the Court. Here the skeletons of two tall men were found, lying close together in the earth. The passage was made eighty to ninety feet in length, under the wall, the court, and the castle; first through earth, then loose chalk, then singularly regular layers of chalk, 4 to 6 in. thick, alternating with thinner bands of flint and chalky gravel; and at last the workmen came to a wall barring their passage. This, with much labour, they forced, and found on the other side of it a room filled with earth, chalk, and rubble. When wholly cleared out, the space was found to be rectangular, about 17 feet by 14 feet, the height over 20 feet. It was immediately below the square-shaped extension of the keep, and its floor lower than the present level of the ground. We were furnished with lights and a ladder, in order to be able to thoroughly examine the walls of this long buried chamber. We found them to be of flint and rubble concrete, except on the south-east, where the wall seemed to consist of squared blocks of hard chalk. On closer scrutiny we found that the chalk wall was but the filling up of a large round archway, the opening of which is 16 ft. 8 in. We traced the arch to the keystone at a height of 19 ft. 6 in. It is turned in slabs of thin stone, which, in the upper part, are alternate with red tiles, very like Roman. Where did this arch lead to? Clearly to the perpendicular face of the tower. Going out once more we found the external wall covered with dense and deep growth of ivy, but there, with some difficulty, the arch could be traced. We returned, and examined the interior with additional interest. We could no longer regard it as being originally a room ; its walls were without window or loop, but the wall opposite to the great arch was pierced by two smaller arches. One of these opens to a low and narrow passage leading into a small spiral staircase, which had also been filled up entirely with earth and rubble. Its walls, steps, and even the newel around which they ascend are built of a very hard flint concrete. This staircase had been abandoned at some period, and was then domed over and blocked up. In it is a very rudely shaped loop, over which a single slab of stone was originally inserted into the concrete. The exterior of this loop must at present lie several feet below the surface of the earth in the court outside. This ancient disused staircase ascended not far from what we have termed the grand staircase. The wall pierced by the two passages is massive, but terminates at a height of about 20 feet, the wall of the tower above crossing it at an angle. The north-east wall of the extension of the keep rests partly on the corresponding wall of this lowest portion, but projects over it considerably. In the floor of this buried place a well was discovered. Its pipe had been continued through the earth into the room above. It would thus appear that the supposed room, which the excavators found in so singular a manner, was probably a court, having a large round arch at its entrance, which gave access to the keep tower.

Returning to the staircase now in use, we pass first into a fine octagon room, which is, in fact, two stories in one. The large window openings of this room have evidently been at some time roughly enlarged, the original openings being probably mere loops. On one side of the room is a fragment of a round column, one of two which flanked a doorway, long since blocked up. A passage has been forced into the square wing of the tower, through a wall 12ft. 6in. thick. The topmost room of the octagonal tower was evidently the chief room. It is well lighted by large round windows, and forms at present a very handsome billiard-room, the prospect from its windows over the surrounding country being magnificent. When and by whom this remarkable keep was built we will not venture to guess. Whether the traditions which have ascribed to the earliest fortress of Chilham a British, a Roman, or a Saxon origin be fact or fable, it is almost certain that a stronghold of some kind was here before Norman barons supplanted Saxon earls as lords of the land.

Camden says that in his time (1586) it was the confirmed opinion of the inhabitants that the Romans had on this spot one of their permanent camps. He believed it to be the site of the battle in which Cæsar lost his tribune Quintus Laberius Durus. Long before Camden visited Chilham, the great barrow, still to be seen on the slope of the hill behind the old French Mill, was called Julaber's or Julaberry's grave. It would, indeed, be a remarkable instance of the persistence of ancient names, strangely corrupted, if the name of this grave mound be, as some have conjectured, derived from Julius and Laberius. The barrow is situated on the south bank of the river opposite the Castle-hill. Its length is about 150ft. and its width 45ft. ; the depth increases as the hill slopes, so that the central line of the top is nearly horizontal ; it is roughly round in section, and the earth of which it is composed seems to be fine and free from pebbles. The barrow was opened in the last century by the Earl of Winchilsey, a cutting having been made across the centre, but no remains were discovered. They would more probably be found in the deepest part at the north end. One of the most interesting of the many ancient earthworks in this district is the earth-circle half-a-mile south east of Chilham, which Mr. Petrie, in his "Notes on Kentish Earthworks," speaks of as " one of the most perfect, regular, and delicately executed works in existence ; nearly equalling the very best of the Wiltshire remains, as it has an average error of under four inches from a true circle, on a diameter of about one hundred and thirty feet."

Chilham Castle was the scene of a memorable meeting between King John and Archbishop Stephen Langton, the Castle being then held by Roesia de Dover, whose second husband was a natural son of the king. Their daughter Isabel married first the Earl of Athol, and subsequently Alexander Baliol, brother of King Baliol, the "Toom Tabard." Isabel de Chilham died at the Castle in 1292, and was buried in the

Crypt of Canterbury Cathedral, where her altar-tomb is one of the most ancient monuments remaining; it bears a recumbent figure of the Countess. Her son John was concerned with Robert Bruce in the murder of the treacherous Red Comyn. Edward I. caused him to be hanged at Canterbury on a gallows fifty feet high, and in order to "make siccar," as Sir Roger Kirkpatrick said, the Earl was beheaded after he was hanged, and his body burnt after that. The Lords of Chilham in those days indulged somewhat freely in treason, for the next one, the rich Lord Badlesmere, was also executed on that charge. Henry VIII. granted the Castle to Sir Thomas Cheney, who added greatly, it is said, to the strength and beauty of the buildings. Sir Thomas must have been a man of changeable humour, however; for, according to Leland, who visited the place in 1552, he soon after pulled down most of the magnificent mansion he had erected, and carried off the materials to build his house at Shurland, in Sheppy. It is to Sir Dudley Digges that we owe the present beautiful mansion. Philipot says he was "A great asserter of his country's liberties in the worst of times," and his epitaph in the church records that "His noble soul could not stoop to ambition." It may be taken as an illustration of what was possible in the "worst of times" that the office of Master of the Rolls was conferred on the knight in spite of the fact that he was entirely ignorant of the law. Sir Dudley's life was an active and varied one. He had sat in Parliament; had been a voyager in the Arctic Seas in search of the north-west passage; had been sent as Ambassador to the barbaric Court of Muscovy; and had been a prisoner in the Fleet Prison before he was raised to the Bench. When he became master of Chilham, he pulled down what was left of the old house, and built on the site of it the beautiful Jacobean mansion which still remains.

Chilham Church, dedicated to St. Mary, consists of a nave and two aisles, a west tower, north and south transepts, and a chancel with side chapels. The nave arcades are each of four pointed arches on octagonal pillars. The tower, erected about 1534, is square, with a beacon turret: it opens by a fine arch to the nave. The ceiling of the nave is flat, some of the original timber spandrels remaining. The aisle and clerestory windows are Perpendicular. The north chapel contains an early piscina. The south transept has a timber roof with king-posts. The transept windows are of the Decorated period, but in no way remarkable. The present spacious chancel is due to the munificence of the late Mr. Charles Hardy, who enlarged and restored this portion of the church. The south pier of the chancel arch contains the door of the Rood screen; it is at present blocked up, but might easily be opened. On the north side of the chancel there was formerly a circular, domed Mausoleum of the Colebrooke family: it was Italian in style, and was removed during the extension of the chancel. Formerly an old chantry stood on the north side of the chancel; it was dissolved in the reign of Edward VI. The Digges chapel on the south side contains the monuments of that family. In the chancel is an exquisite monument, by Chantrey, to the late Mr. James Wildman, of Chilham Castle.

The Digges monument is a " Jacob's pillar" which Sir Dudley set up over the grave of his lady. Its square pedestal has epitaphs on the knight and his lady, in the exaggerated style of eulogy which prevailed in the seventeenth century. Around the black marble pillar are figures representing the cardinal virtues. A later inscription traces back the Digges family to "John Digge" who gave the island of "Bynwith" to the Grey Friars. Sir Dudley died in 1638. At the west end of the church is a monument of Bethersden marble, the surface beautifully ornamented with flat scroll-work. It is to the memory of Lady Palmer, sister of Sir Dudley Digges. A similarly decorated monument in the Digges Chancel, to one of the Fagge family, has a very quaint epitaph. There are several other monuments of interest in this church.

CHAPTER XXI.

Nackington, Bridge, Bishopsbourne.

BOUT a mile south-east from Canterbury, and standing apart from the high road, is the little church of St. Mary, Nackington. It consists of a nave, chancel, and south chapel, with a small square tower at the north-west corner of the nave; it has a south door and a north porch. The roof is timbered, the old tie-beams and king-posts remaining in sound condition.

Some of the windows are early Norman, small, without moulding, and deeply splayed internally; others are Early English lancets; the east window is a modern double lancet, filled with stained glass, and dedicated to the memory of Richard and Hannah Mount. The south chapel, which is divided from the chancel by a low, wide, unbroken, pointed arch, has a two-light window, containing some fragments of old glass. The north wall of the chancel has two pointed recesses, one evidently an aumbry. In the east pier of the chapel arch there is another recess, in which was, no doubt, a piscina, and beside it what was probably another aumbry. There are no brasses, but the chapel contains several mural monuments of the Milles family, and there are in the floor of the church tomb-stones which date back to the 17th century. Several members of the Godfrey-Faussett family are buried in the church and churchyard, amongst them the learned author of "Inventorium Sepulchrale," the Rev. Bryan Faussett, of Heppington. Here also lies his descendant, the late Mr. Godfrey-Faussett, a genial and accomplished antiquary, author of "Canterbury till Domesday," We recognised in the memorial cross which stands above his grave, a copy of that interesting cross found near St. Martin's churchyard, of the discovery of which Bryan Faussett wrote a century before. Even the style of the ancient inscription has been followed. Close to the church is a farm-house, which was originally the court lodge of the manor of Sextries, the name a corruption of Sacristy, the manor having been appropriated to the use of the Sacrist of St. Augustine's Monastery. Heppington is another manor in this parish. Among its ancient owners were the Chiche's, the Fagge's, and the Hales's; subsequently it was possessed by the Godfrey's, from the last of whom it passed to his son-in-law, the Bryan Faussett above mentioned. Nackington house, another old mansion in this parish, was, during the Stuart period, the residence of the Nutt family, of whom several are buried at Nackington. It was at a later date the residence of the Milles family.

Next to Nackington in our circuit around the city, we come to Bridge, on the main road to Dover—the old Roman road or Watling Street. It is about two-and-a-half miles from Canterbury, and is the largest of a series of villages within the valley of the Lesser Stour or Bourne. Several of these, situated in the midst of sylvan and pastoral scenery of great beauty, and having churches which possess features of interest, lie within easy access from Canterbury.

Bridge Church, dedicated to St. Peter, has always been regarded as a chapel to Patrixbourne, although Bridge gives its name to the deanery and to the hundred. The ancient manor of Bridge or Blackmansbury belonged, like Nackington, to the Sacristy of St. Augustine's Abbey. Some time after its alienation it was held, in 1638, by Sir Arnold Braems, a descendant of an old Flemish family. He built there the splendid mansion of Bridge Place, the greater part of which was in the early part of the seventeenth century pulled down by John Taylor, the first of that name who was squire of Bifrons. The manor of Beracre, or Baracre, in Bridge parish is supposed to have given a name to the family of Bargar, or Bargrave, long resident in the village. The Register of Bridge records the baptism, in 1580, of "Isaacke Bargar," to which a note has been added, "Afterwards Deane of Canterbury."

Bridge Church (St. Peter's), though it has undergone extensive restoration, still retains many signs of its antiquity. It has a nave, two aisles, chancel, north transept, and south-west tower with spire. The most ancient portions of the church are—the plain round headed and deeply splayed windows of the tower and of the chancel, and those of the east end of the south aisle; the west door which has a bold round moulding, square capitals with billet ornament and circular shafts, and hood-moulding with tooth-ornament and head terminals; the small round headed door with chevron mouldings on the east of the north transept, and which is certainly not in its original position—all these are Norman. Other portions of the church are Early English, including the lancet windows of the north aisle and the north transept. The rest of the church has been so much altered as to make it difficult to ascertain what it was before it passed under the restorer's hands. The chancel arch was probably Early English; the plain pointed arches of the north aisle arcade are of that period, but their piers have been removed and double round pillars substituted. The windows other than those mentioned are various in style, and call for no comment. The north wall of the chancel contains a very curious piece of ancient sculpture, within the tympanum of a round arch. The upper part, which is very much defaced, apparently represented Our Lord seated on clouds of glory. Below this is a band of five panels, illustrative of the Fall, and of the first murder. The 2nd represents the Temptation by the Serpent; the 1st the Expulsion from Eden; the 3rd and 4th the offerings of Cain and Abel, the 5th the murder of Abel. There is in the same wall of the chancel an interesting painting of Richard Bargrave, of Bridge, gent. obt. 1649. Within the altar rails, on the same side, there is a recess containing the life-sized figure of a man, most singularly divided into two halves by a central pier. Above this there is a brass plate commemorative of the two wives of the builder of Bridge Place. It says:—" Joane, second daughter of Walter Harflet of Beakesbourne, lieth buried in the parish church of Dover: Elizabeth, second daughter of Sir Dudley Diggs, Master of the Rolls, second wife of Sir Arnold Braems, lieth buried in the middle of this chancel." In the same wall there are two shields, one with armorial bearings, the other with the emblems of mortality, the skull, cross bones, pick and spade, nicely carved in marble. The south wall contains some very singular memorial devices, with scrolls bearing inscriptions in Latin, the lettering Old English. Hasted says one of these is in memory of " Macobus Kasey," Vicar of Patricksbourne during 21 years. We could not see to decipher the inscription, but Canon Scott Robertson, in his account of the Vicars of Patricksbourne, says it is a memorial to Malcolm Ramsey, M.A., who died in 1538, having held the living for forty-four years. The church has an open timbered roof. The lower part of the tower forms a Baptistery.

Bourne Park is just beyond Bridge. The miniature river flows through it and expands into a small lake in front of the mansion, behind which a mass of fine timber connects the park with Gorsley Wood. Although it lies beyond the first circle of villages from Canterbury, we cannot resist the temptation to cross the park to the little village of Bishopsbourne, the peaceful home in which Hooker lived his gentle, learned, pious life, planting those grand yew hedges which still enclose his garden, and writing the great work on Ecclesiastical Polity which will outlive the yews.

Bishopsbourne church has a nave and chancel, without chancel arch; a chapel south of the chancel; a north chapel divided from the nave by two pointed arches, with an octagonal pillar, the abacus of which is square; a south transept, also with two pointed arches, has a round pillar, the capital of which is square. The chancel has an east window, of five lights, which contains the arms of Hooker, and of Archbishop Howley. The two-light side windows, with Decorated tracery, contain modern stained glass. The chancel walls have recently been faced with beautiful glass tiles, and a handsome reredos in three panels of mosaic, contains the representation of the Transfiguration. In the south wall is a piscina, the back of which is diapered with a pattern of quatrefoils. The chancel contains the monument of Richard Hooker. There is a rood door in a pier on the south side. There anciently stood, within a recess in the church, an image of the Virgin, the pedestal of which was a famous relic, for it is recorded that, in 1462, one William Hawte bequeathed to the church this stone as a piece of that on which the Archangel Gabriel descended when he saluted the Virgin. The north doorway is Early English and has outside, on the left hand of it, a pointed stoup; the tower at the west end is in the Perpendicular style, with three stages, and an octagonal staircase-turret. The church contains several monuments and memorial windows of interest.

The Rector (the Rev. T. Hirst), very kindly showed us the ancient rooms of the Rectory, the study of the "Judicious Hooker," which was also the room in which the great scholar died in 1600. This room has a fine ceiling, richly panelled in oak. We were able also, to inspect the old parchment register containing his signatures. Some unscrupulous hunter after autographs deliberately cut out one of them a few years back. The yew-tree hedges which Hooker planted nearly three hundred years ago are flourishing still, and have grown to an immense size; they are looked after with the greatest care.

CHAPTER XXII.

Patricksbourne, Bekesbourne, and Littlebourne.

SHORT walk from Bridge along the bank of the Bourne, by Bifrons Park, brings us to Patricksbourne, one of the most picturesque of Kentish villages. It was originally called Bourne only, the prefix Patrick's being probably derived from one of the owners of the manor in the 13th or 14th century. The church is mentioned in Domesday, but much of the present building was probably erected in the next century. It consisted, before its enlargement, of a nave and chancel, with a south aisle bisected by a tower forming a porch, a very rare arrangement. The porch has one of the finest Norman doorways known. It was the opinion of the late Sir Gilbert Scott that it was considered to be too beautiful to be removed, and the later tower was built over it. The round arch of the door has three tiers of moulding, with carved capitals on round shafts. The tympanum contains a sculptured representation of Our Lord with attendant angels. The enrichment of the mouldings is remarkably varied and elaborate. It consists of foliage, human and animal heads, grotesque birds and beasts, and smaller ornaments very delicately carved. Above the tympanum is a tall canopy, which contains a semi-circular niche, within which is the *Agnus Dei*. The tower has three bells; the oldest bears the inscription, "Ave Maria gracia plena." The other two were cast by Palmer, of Canterbury, in 1674.

The tower has one round arch opening to the west part of the aisle, its other two arches being pointed. The Chancel arch is somewhat of horse-shoe shape, and rests on slender shafts. The east end has a fine wheel-window of eight lights, the mouldings chevroned. Below this is a triplet of narrow round-headed windows, the middle one higher than the others. On each side wall of the Chancel are two small and plain Norman windows. The Chancel contains two aumbries, and an early piscina with a crocketed canopy. There is also a squint from the south aisle. The Priest's door in the south of the chancel has a rich carving of early Norman work, with handsome capitals and shafts. On the north side of the church there is another Norman doorway, which was moved to its present position when the north aisle was built in 1824. The chancel window contains some Flemish glass of the 16th century, collected by the first Marchioness Conyngham.

The mansion of Bifrons, the Kent seat of the Marquis Conyngham, was erected by John Bargrave, brother of Dean Bargrave. The Latin epitaph of John Bargrave in Patricksbourne Church states that the family stood and fell with the cause of the King in the Civil Wars. The grandson of the first builder of Bifrons was obliged to part with the estate, almost immediately after the Restoration, to Sir Arthur Slingsby. In 1694 it was sold to Mr. John Taylor, in whose family it remained until the beginning of the present century. In 1767, the Rev. Edward Taylor succeeded to the estate, and was also vicar of the parish. He pulled down the old mansion, and built the present one close to the old site.

Bifrons Park contains the site of one of the most extensive Saxon cemeteries in this part of Kent. In 1866 some workmen, digging for a new plantation on Patricksbourne Hill, found a few Saxon graves, and in the autumn of 1867, Mr. T. G. Godfrey-Faussett, having obtained permission from the Marquis to excavate, discovered the principal cemetery, half way up the slope of the hill, on the south-eastern side of the valley, and about 200 yards from the Dover road; more than a hundred graves were opened, and a very valuable and interesting collection of Saxon antiquities was formed; this is now preserved at Bifrons. During the present year, the Rev. F. T. Vine, vicar of Patricksbourne, has opened up some additional barrows in Gorsley Wood.

Bekesbourne, which is next Patricksbourne, is a small parish containing less than a square mile. It is remarkable, as having been since a very early period, an outlying limb of the Cinque Port of Hastings, and a court of Shepway, for the Cinque Port Jurisdiction has been held here. Hasted says that the Mayor of Hastings formerly appointed one of the principal inhabitants of Bekesbourne to act as his deputy, but that the custom having been discontinued, "the natives are in consequence necessitated to journey upwards of fifty miles in order to obtain redress in cases of emergency, so that the district, from that inconvenience, has become an ungovernable and lawless tract of country." Happily all that has changed, and a better order prevails. The parish takes its name from the family of Beke, who held the manor some time after the Conquest. In earlier times it was called Living or Livingsbourne. The parish is less than a square mile in extent. Its church, dedicated to St. Peter, is prettily situated on the slope of the hill which rises towards Adisham downs. It has a nave, chancel, and south transept, with small west tower, the latter a specimen of the "Churchwarden Gothic" of 1814. The north door is Norman. Its outer arch has courses of chevrons, the recessed arch mouldings being a round and hollow. The capitals are all different in style of ornament, two of them having rudely formed heads with other carvings. The hood-moulding has tooth-ornament, and terminates in masks. Two small Norman windows on either side of the chancel can be seen externally, but they have long been filled up. The chancel contains several lancet windows; its east window is a double lancet, deeply splayed, and with three exceedingly fine Early English brackets on the piers. Below the string course, and immediately behind the altar, are two niches, now concealed by the dorsal hangings. One has apparently been an aumbry; the other is smaller, and has an early trefoiled moulding. In the south wall is an interesting double piscina, within a deep rectangular recess, divided by an octagonal pillar. Close to the north door is a pointed stoup. The south transept is used as a vestry. Its walls contain some monuments of interest; one is to Sir Thomas Pym Hales, Bart., "A Representative of the Borough of Dover, and a true friend to Liberty and the laws of his country." He died in 1773. Another has this inscription, "Here lyeth ye body of Richard Fogg, Esq., descended of ye ancient family of ye Foggs of this county:

he sarved King Charles ye First as Captaine at Sea. Afterwards he retired himselfe to a private life in this parish and attained unto ye 81st yeare of his age." He died in 1681. In the tower, removed from the chancel, is a fine marble monument of Sir Henry Palmer, who died in 1611. The knight is clad in armour, and is kneeling in the act of prayer. In the floor of the church is a stone, with a brass plate bearing a Latin epitaph on Henry Porredge, 1593, written by himself. Here also is the grave of Nicholas Battely, Vicar of Bekesbourne and Rector of Ivychurch, the learned editor of Somner. He died in 1704. Several of the family were buried here.

The church has recently been restored. It anciently appertained to the Priory of St. Gregory, but since the Dissolution it has been in the patronage of the Archbishop. In 1314 a chantry was founded in it by James de Bourne, then lord of the manor. The Registers of Bekesbourne are well preserved. They commence in 1558, when the name is spelt Beakesboorne. At the end of the book is a list of vicars, apparently copied from an older record. The first name is thus given:— "William de St. Edmundo, Rector de Living, 1250." The church plate includes an ancient chalice of silver, engraved. The body appears to have been restored, but the lid contains an inscription—" BEKSHORN IN A N^o. D^mi 1578."

Opposite the church is an old mansion known as Beke House. This was the site of an archiepiscopal palace. The manor of Bekesbourne becoming the property of Archbishop Chicheley, was transferred by him to Christ Church. Prior Goldstone, in the reign of Henry VII., enlarged the mansion, and erected a chapel, hall, and other buildings there. On the fall of the monastery, the manor and the prior's mansion passed into lay hands; but Archbishop Cranmer soon after obtained it by exchange for the manor of Bishopsbourne, and made it one of his palaces. It is said to have been the favourite residence of Archbishop Parker. Very little trace remains of the old palace, which was sacked by the roundheads in the Civil War. A memorial of Cranmer's connection with it is left in a wall of the present buildings, viz., his arms, with his initials and motto: "T. C. 1552. Nosce te ipsum et Deum."

Between Bekesbourne and Littlebourne we pass Howlets or Owlets, the seat to which, in 1620, Sir Charles Hales removed from Thanington. The mansion had been previously the residence of the Sir Henry Palmer, whose effigy is in Bekesbourne church. While the Hales's lived there the old house fell down, and the estate was sold to Isaac Baugh, Esq., who built a new house near the site of the former one. There are some very fine beeches in the grounds.

Littlebourne is distant about two miles from Bekesbourne and five from Canterbury. It is a long straggling village, with the church lying at the outskirt. The manor of Littlebourne anciently belonged to St. Augustine's Monastery, its vineyards being planted there, while somewhat nearer to the city, at the place now known as Fishpool-bottom, the monks had their fish-ponds. The church, which is dedicated to St. Vincent, is mainly Early English. It consists of a nave, two aisles, and chancel, with a west tower. The exterior has a singular outline, the chancel roof being considerably higher than that of the nave. There is a south doorway with slender round pillars and capitals, the mouldings of the first pointed period. No one could suppose from the outside that this door is blocked up inside with masonry. The west door in the tower is also pointed, but plain. The chief feature of the church is its lofty Early English chancel. The east window is a beautiful triple lancet deeply splayed, with the hood-moulding springing from slender round columns. Each side has four splayed lancet windows, and in the whole chancel nothing is incongruous. The eleven lancets have all been filled with stained glass memorial windows. The east triplet, which represents the Nativity, Crucifixion, and Burial of our Lord, is in memory of the late Henry Kingsford, Esq., obt. 1866, æt. 73. The south windows contain the Evangelists; two windows were dedicated by the late Vicar (The Rev. F. Rouch); two were given by Denne Denne, Esq., in memory of his wife and third daughter. The northern windows have the Prophets Isaiah, Jeremiah, Ezekiel and Daniel. They are memorial windows to Mary and Richard Pembrook, Mary Gardener, and Frederic Swaine. In the south wall is an early-pointed piscina with two basins. Above the string course on the north side is a square aumbry with an old oaken door. The chancel arch is early pointed; its pillars are curiously encased in wood. The nave arcade on the south side has five Early English arches resting on wall piers. There was probably a corresponding arcade on the north side, one of the original arches of which may be seen on the outside wall of the nave, where a two-light window has been inserted. When the present north aisle was erected, the arcade on that side was formed of two large and disproportioned round arches, quite out of style with the general building. In the east wall of this aisle is a two-light pointed window which is probably older than the aisle itself. There is a memorial window to Captain James and his wife. The south aisle has one lancet, and a later two-light window which is filled with stained glass; one light in memory of Henry Denne, 1822, and the other of the Ven. John Denne, Archdeacon of Rochester, born at Littlebourne, 1693, buried at Rochester, 1707. The tower has a lancet which is also filled with stained glass. In the chancel is a flat stone bearing the arms of De L'Angle, in a widow's lozenge, and the inscription Elizabeth De L'Angle, died June vii., 1750. In the east respond of the south aisle arcade the Rood door is still seen.

CHAPTER XXIII.

Fordwich and Sturry.

OLLOWING the circle of parishes which join those of the city, we next come to Fordwich, a very ancient place, which, with the population of a small village, still enjoys the dignity of a corporate borough. In Domesday it is named Forewic. It is a limb of the Cinque Port of Sandwich. The town was, no doubt, an important place in the remote times when there was a broad estuary between the mainland and Thanet, and the tidal way was open to Reculver. The Corporation of Fordwich consists of a Mayor, Jurats, and Freemen. The Mayor is also Coroner, and the jurats are justices. There is a Town Hall, in which the magistrates hold sessions, and administer justice. They are not wholly without the means of executing judgment, for below the Court-hall is the lock-up. There was, until the last century, a gallows by the quay; and there is still preserved—though no longer used—the ancient ducking-stool for termagant wives. The Corporation has its insignia; the mace is a fine specimen, silver gilt and richly ornamented. It was a present from Admiral Graydon, who served with Sir George Rooke in the storming of Vigo. Both of these veterans retired to spend their last days near Canterbury. The Graydons had long been resident at Fordwich, and in the old mansion there the gallant Admiral died in 1727. Among the ancient privileges of the jurats was the right to take each a night-turn at netting the delicious trout for which the Stour was so renowned.

Fordwich gave a territorial title to two peerages. Sir John Finch, recorder of Canterbury, and member for that city, was chosen Speaker in the Parliament of 1628. It was he who was kept in the Chair by force while the House passed the resolutions against the King's oppressive demands. During the long interval in which Charles I. dispensed with a Parliament Sir John Finch was made Chief Justice of the Common Pleas, being a zealous supporter of the King in his exactions. He was created Lord Finch, Baron Fordwich. Being impeached by the Long Parliament he was obliged to escape to Holland. He returned at the Restoration, and took part in the trial of the Regicides, but soon after died, and was buried at St. Martin's, Canterbury. Lord Cowper, on elevation to an earldom in 1718, was created Viscount Fordwich.

The Church of St. Mary is an ancient structure, with a nave, north aisle, and chancel. Three early-pointed arches divide the nave from the aisle; the chancel aisle and the tower arch are also pointed. The windows are later. There are some curious inscriptions on the ancient grave-stones in the floor of the church. One dated 1605 is in memory of Aphra, wife of Henry Hawkins, "who scarcely having arrived to 21 years of age yet fully attayned perfection in many vertues" ere she "departed this frayle life." The epitaph of Catherine, wife of Valentine Norton of Fordwich, gent, also records an early death. She died in 1610, in her 21st year. The following lines are upon her tombstone :—

> Fame soundes so shrill over this tender coarse,
> The dead growne deafe and Fame herselfe growne hoarse.
> Malicious Envye cannot carpe at Fame ;
> For what she soundes the dead deserv'd the same.
> All speake her worth that knewe her mayde or wife :
> Let all speake, all too little to her life.
> Fate is excus'd : it robs not her of bliss,
> But us that such a lively mirrour miss.
> One onely sonne she bore, at whose deare byrth
> She changed her earthlye joyes to Heavenlye mirth.

There is in the church an ancient stone shrine, ark shaped, the roof carved with overlapping scallops, and one side with a series of small interlacing round arches, springing from round columns. This shrine has been for some years exposed to the weather, on the outside of the church. Hasted says it was originally inside, but was cast out into the churchyard, where it was likely to be destroyed. It was purchased by someone who removed it to the Precincts of Canterbury Cathedral. From there it was brought back, some years since, to Fordwich churchyard, and has now, quite recently, been once again taken within the church—its proper place. Its original history is not known.

On the opposite side of the Stour, close to Fordwich, is the village of Sturry (the Stour isle). At the time of the Domesday survey there was a much greater extent of river area in the parish. "Esturai," as it was then called, had only 28 acres of meadow land, but it had no less than ten mills and seven fisheries on the Stour. Sturry Court, now a farm, is an old mansion house of the time of James I. The present building contains part of the original, but has been much altered. The entrance has still the ancient gate archway. The manor of Sturry was, in the reign of Elizabeth, sold by John Tufton to Thomas Smythe, of Westenhanger, who was also owner of the manor of Barton, at Canterbury. He was the Mr. "Customer" Smythe, named in the curious deposition of the Aldermen of Canterbury, concerning the breaking up of a part of Babb's Hill, Canterbury, by one Robert Young. The Customer's grandson, Sir Thomas Smythe, was created, in 1628, Viscount Strangford. The Strangfords appear to have resided at Sturry Court, but in 1700, on the death of the Viscount Strangford of that time, the estate passed to his son-in-law, Henry Roper, Lord Teynham.

Sturry Church (St. Nicholas), is large and interesting. It has a nave, chancel, two aisles, and west tower. It has passed through many changes since its earliest walls were built. Above the four Early English, plain-pointed arches, on square piers, forming the nave arcade on either side, circular arches can be seen, apparently the remains of clerestory windows of a Norman building. The chancel was probably built during the transition to the first pointed style. Its east window has two lancets, trefoiled. There is an aumbry in the north, and a piscina in the south wall. The present windows of the church are mostly of second or third pointed style. The roof has tie-beams and king-posts. The chancel arch is pointed. There is a new oak screen. One of the pillars of the south aisle has a pointed niche; the same aisle has an early-pointed piscina. On the west wall of this aisle is a stone tablet with inscription recording the burial, in 1544, of Katherine, wife of Johne Churche. In the floor is a flat stone with a brass, the Latin inscription on which commemorates Thomas Childmel, of Sturry, and his two wives, Joan and Katherine. He gave lead for the roofing of the church to the value of £40, and in other ways proved a benefactor to the parish; he died in 1496. The north aisle has a square aumbry enlarged internally. The north porch, with a good timber-framed roof, apparently dates from the Tudor period. The west tower is square and opens to the nave by a pointed arch.

NOTE TO CHAPTER II.—Since this chapter was printed, further discoveries have been made at St. Martin's, in connection with the two ancient arches illustrated on page 8. The internal wall has been laid bare, and the round arch exposed on the inside, corresponding exactly to that on the exterior. The flat headed arch, which has been a subject of so much speculation, was found to contain a squint, the slope of which was inclined to the *west*, as though directed to a side altar.

INDEX.

Abbot, Archbishop, 55
Albinus, Abbot of St. Augustine's, 23
Alcock, Capt. William, St. Stephen's, 84
Alford, Dean, St. Martin's, 14
All Saints', 94
Alms-box, ancient, Harbledown, 56
Altar, ancient, at St. Pancras, 18
Anabaptists, 106
Archer, Peter, Chartham, 124
Arundel, Archbishop, 79
Athol, Countess of, Chilham, 131
Athol, Earl of, 132
Attwood, Thos., St. Mildred's, 70
Augustine Friars, 108
Augustine, his landing in Kent, 5; his settlement at Canterbury, 6; his simple life, 21; his remains translated to the Abbey Church, 25
Badlesmere, Lord, Chilham, 132
Baldwin, Archbishop, 79, 88
Bargrave (Bargar) family, 135, 124
Barham, Rev. R. H., 76
Barrows, Chartham Downs, 123; Chilham, 131; Iffin, 115
Barton, Elizabeth, St. Sepulchre's, 110
Batteley, Nicholas, Bekesbourne, 142
Beauvoir, Dr., "Liber Hospitalium," 50
Becket, "relics" at Harbledown, 56
Bede, his account of St. Martin's, 3
Beke House, 142
Bekesbourne, a limb of Hastings, 141; The Church, 140
Beresford-Hope, Mr., 29, 31
Bertha, Queen, her Oratory at St. Martin's, 3; her so-called tomb, 11; buried at St. Augustine's, 12, 22
Bifrons Park, 140
Bigbury Wood, ancient camp, 115
Bigg William, St. George's Gate, 99
Binnewith Island, 107
Bishopsbourne, 137
Black Friars, The, 104
Black Prince, at Harbledown, 54
Blue Dick (Culmer), 126

"Bob-up-and-down," Chaucer's, 121
Bolaine, Betty, Burgate Church, 75
Bourne, Abbot de, 23
Bourne, James de, Bekesbourne, 142
Bourne Park, 137
Boys, Sir John, Jesus Hospital, 112
Braems, Sir Arnold, Bridge, 135
Brasses—St. Martin's, 13; St. George's, 75; Burgate, 75; St. Paul's, 76; St. Dunstan's, 86; St. Alphage, 93; Northgate, 93; Thanington, 114; Chartham, 125; Bridge, 136; Bekesbourne, 142; Sturry, 148
Bridewell, the old, 109
Bridge, The Church, 135; Manor, 135
Bridger family, St. Mildred's, 69
British camps, near Canterbury, 115
Brock, Mr. Loftus, on St. Martin's font, 13
Brown, Ralph, Northgate Church, 93
Bungeye, Rev. John, Chartham, 126
Burgate, or Borough Gate, 101
Burgate Church, 75
Burnt House, The, Chartham, 124
Canuto's gifts to St. Augustine's, 27
Canterbury, in Saxon times, 2; sacked by the Danes, 24; Scholarships at Cambridge, 62
Castle, The, 95
Caxton, John, St. Alphage, 93
Cemeteries, ancient, St. Sepulchre's, 111
Change ringers, St. Stephen's, 81
Chantries—Harbledown, 54; St. Paul's, 76; St. Dunstan's, 86; Holy Cross, 89; Chilham, 133; Bekesbourne, 142
Charles I. at St. Augustine's, 40
Charters of St. Augustine's, 26
Chartham—The Church, 124; Deanery, 124; Saxon Cemetery, 123
Chaucer's "Bob-up-and-down," 57, 121
Cheney, Sir Thomas, Chilham, 132
Chequers, Chaucer's Inn, 59
Chesshyre, Rev. W. J., 11, 77
Chiches family, 94, 135

INDEX.

Childmel, Thomas, 148
Chilham, The Castle, 128; Romans at, 131; The Church, 132
Chrismatory found at St. Martin's, 14
Churche, John, Sturry, 148
Cogan's Hospital, 112
Cokyn (Cockyn), William, 59, 67
Colebrooke family, Chilham, 133
Colepepper, Colonel, Hackington, 79
Coleridge, Bishop, St. Augustine's, 41
Coleridge, Rev. Ed., St. Augustine's, 40
Colet, Dean, at Harbledown, 56
Colfe, Abraham, Westgate, 90
Conyngham family, Bifrons, 140
Cotton, Leonard, 74; his Hospital, 112
Cranmer family, St. Mildred's, 67
Cranmer, Archbishop, and the Blackfriars, 106; his palace at Bekesbourne, 142
Cross, ancient, found at St. Martin's, 13, 135; The Iron, 73
Culmer (Blue Dick), 126
Dane John, The, 96
De L'Angle, Rector of Chartham, 124
Denne, Archdeacon, Littlebourne, 144
Diggs, John, Greyfriars, 107
Digges, Sir Dudley, Chilham, 132
Doge, Hamo, St. Paul, 76
Dole, Villai, St. George's, 75
Dominican Friars, 104
Ducking stool, Fordwich, 145
Dunstan, St. Augustine's, 22
Eadbald, his apostacy, 22
Earth-circle at Chilham, 131
Eastbridge Hospital, 58
Elizabeth, Queen, at St. Augustine's, 43
Elmar, Abbot, and the Danes, 24
Erasmus, at Harbledown, 56
Essex, John, Abbot, St. Augustine's, 26
Ethelbert, his palace, 2; buried at St. Augustine, 12; his temple, 15, 18; his second marriage, 22
Ethelbert's Tower, 31, 34
Exchange, ancient, in Canterbury, 60
Fagge family, Chilham, 133, 135
Farnham, John, Eastbridge Hospital, 62
Faussett, Bryan Rev., on the cross at St. Martin's, 13; his "Inventorium Sepulchrale," 123; Nackington, 134
Fferne, David, dwarf, St. Paul's, 77
Finch, Sir John, 146
Fineux, George, St. Paul's, 76
Fishpool-bottom, 143
Flints, squared, 42

Fogg, Richard, Bekesbourne, 141
Font—ancient, St. Martin's, 13; St. Pancras, 16; St. John's, 47; St. George's, 75
Ford, at Thanington, 115
Fordwich, 27, 145
Fraternity of Jesus Masse, 89
,, Parish Clerks, 106
Fulks, Stephen and Alice, 13
Furley, John, St. Stephen's, 84
Furley, William Henry, 77
Fyndon, Abbot, St. Augustine's, 37
Gallows—St. Dunstan's, 88; Westgate, 90; Fordwich, 145
Gates, City, 97
Gibbons, Orlando, at Canterbury, 40
Gilbert Canon, a choir boy, 40
Gray, William, Burgate Church, 76
Gray, The poet, at Canterbury, 113
Graydon, Admiral, 145
Gregory, Pope, and Augustine, 5
Grey Friars (Franciscans), 107
Guy, of Warwick, Harbledown, 57
Hackington, Tournament at, 79
Hales family, St. Augustine's, 26; St. Stephen's, 79; Thanington, 116; Bekesbourne, 141, 143
Hales, Sir James, Tonford, 116
Hales' Place, 81
Hales, Sir Thomas Pym, Bekesbourne, 141
Hall, Rev. H., St. John's, 50
Halle, Thomas, brass at Thanington, 114
Harbledown, 52
Harflet, Walter, 136
Hatch, Joseph, married at St. Paul's, 77
Hawte, William, Bishopsbourne, 137
Head, Sir Francis, St. Mildred's, 69
Henry II., at Harbledown, 54
,, St. Dunstan's, 85
Henry of Canterbury, St. Dunstan's, 86
Heppington, 135
Holy Cross Church, Westgate, 89
Holy Maid of Kent, 110
Honywood family, St. Mildred's, 69
Hooker, Richard, Bishopsbourne, 137
Horton Manor, 123
Hospitals—St. John's, 45; St. Nicholas (Harbledown), 51; East Bridge, 58; Poor Priest's, 109; St. Lawrence, 110; St. James', 111; Jesus, 112; Cogan's, 112; Cotton's, 112; Maynard's, 112
Howlets, near Bekesbourne, 143
Hussey, Mr., on St. Mildred's, 66

INDEX.

Iffin, British camp at, 115
"Ingoldsby" (Rev. R. H. Barham), 76, 123
Ingworth, Bishop of Dover, 109
Iron Cross, 73
Jacob, Dr., Wincheap Gate, 98
Jesus Hospital, Northgate, 112
Jesus Masse, Fraternity of, 89
Jews, imprisoned in the Castle, 96
John, King, at Chilham, 131
Julaber's grave, Chilham, 131
Kent, Kings of, St. Augustine's, 24
Kingsford family, Chartham, 124
Klook, Christopher, 76
Lady Wootton's Green, 28
Lanfranc, Archbishop, 45, 49, 50, 52, 85
Langton, Simon, 79, 109
Langton, Stephen, Archbishop, 58, 78, 104
Laurentius, St. Augustine's, 22
Leper Hospitals 45, 52, 110, 112
Leprosy in England, 52
Littlebourne, 143
Living, Livingsbourne, Bekesbourne, 142
Longport, 76, 101
Lovelace family, Greyfriars, 107
Lovelle, John, Priest, St. George's, 75
Luidhard, Chaplain to Queen Bertha, 3
Manwood, Sir Roger, 79, 82, 108
Martyn, John, Graveney Church, 83
Martyr's Field, Wincheap, 103
Mascoll, Robert, St. John's, 49
Maynard's Hospital, 112
Mazer-bowl, ancient, at Harbledown, 56
Mellitus, St. Augustine's, 23
Milles family, 134
Milton Manor, 122
Miracle Plays, Holy Cross Church, 90
Monastery, the first English, 21
More, Sir Thomas, St. Dunstan's, 86
Mystole Park, 127
Nackington, 134
Newingate (St. George's), 99
Newman, Sir George, St. Margaret's, 73
Nolan, Nicholas, Westgate, 90
Norman piscina, St. Martin's, 10
Northgate, 93, 102
Nun of St. Sepulchre's, 110
Nunneries, 104
Nutt family, Nackington, 135
Paintings, ancient, Eastbridge, 63; of Thanington, 116; Bridge, 136
Palmer, Lady, Chilham, 133
Palmer, Sir Henry, Bekesbourne, 142
Paper Mill, Chartham, 124
Parker, Archbishop, 49, 60, 62, 142

Patricksbourne (Patrixbourne), 139
Penny Pot Wood, 127
Petit family, 127
Pierre, Peter de La, 106
Pilgrims' Hall, Eastbridge, 58
Pilgrims' Way, The, 51
Pole, Cardinal, St. Augustine's, 26
Poor Priests' Hospital, 107, 109
Porredge, Henry, Bekesbourne, 142
Priories, 104
Prison at St. Dunstan's, 88; The Castle, 96; Westgate, 103
Prude, Thomas, St. Alphage, 93
Queeningate, 101
Ramsay, Sir Harry, Burgate Church, 75
Ramsey, Malcolm, Patricksbourne, 137
Riding Gate, 99
Roman remains—St. Martin's, 10; St. Pancras, 18; St. Mildred's, 66; Riding Gate, 99
Rondeau family, St. Dunstan's, 81
Rooke's duel, 77
Rooke, Sir George, St. Paul's, 77
Rooke, Sir William, St. Paul's, 77
Roos, Thos. de, Chilham, 60
Roper family, St. Dunstan's, 86, 147
Routledge, Canon, St. Martin's, 10
St. Alphege, 92
St. Andrew's, 94
St. Augustine's, Foundation of the Monastery, 21; rededication by Dunstan, 22; Kings of Kent buried at, 24; Spared by the Danes, 24; Partly destroyed by fire, 25; Occasional distress, 26; Dissolution of the Monastery, 26; The Grand Gate, 28; The ruins of the Abbey, 33; A palace of Henry VIII., 26, 34; A local Vauxhall, 38; Royal visitors to, 40; College, foundation of, 29; College, Dr. Neale's poem on, 30
St. Dunstan's Church, 85
" Place (Roper House), 86
" Edmund, Ridingate, 99
" George's Church, 74
" Gate 99
" Gregory's Priory, 50, 109
" James's (St. Jacob's), Hospital, 111
" John's Hospital, 45
" John the Poor, 71
" Lawrence, Hospital of, 110
" Margaret's Church, 72
" Martin's Church, 9
" Porch, St. Augustine's, 31

INDEX.

St. Mary, Bishopsbourne, 137
,, Bredman, 94
,, Bredin, 94
,, de Castro, 71, 96
,, Chartham, 124
,, Chilham, 132
,, Fordwich, 146
,, Magdalen, Burgate, 75
,, Nackington, 134
,, Northgate, 93
,, Patricksbourne, 140
,, Queeningate, 102
St. Michael's Gate (Burgate), 101
St. Mildred, her relics removed to St. Augustine's, 27
St. Mildred's Church, 65
,, Porch at St. Augustine's, 31
St. Nicholas, Brotherhood of, 106
,, Harbledown, 57
,, Sturry, 147
,, Thanington, 113
St. Pancras, 6, 15
St. Paul's Church, 76
St. Peter, Bekesbourne, 141
,, Bridge, 135
,, Canterbury, 91
St. Sepulchre's Nunnery, 99, 110
St. Stephen's, Hackington, 78
St. Vincent, Littlebourne, 143
Saxon Cemetery, Chartham Downs, 123
,, Bifrons Park, 140
Saxon Masonry at St. Martin's, 10
Scotland, Abbot of St. Augustine's, 25
Septvans, Sir Robert de, Chatham, 125;
    Sir William de, 116
Sertivoli, Michael Francis, 13
Sextries, manor of, Nackington, 135
Shalmsford Street, manor of, 127
Sheldon, Archbishop, 55
Shrine, ancient, Fordwich, 146
Simmons, Alderman, 70
Six, James, M.A., Westgate Church, 90

Smythe, Mr. Customer, 147
Somner, John, Harbledown, 55
Somner, William, St. Margaret's, 73
SS, Collar of, St. Stephen's, 82
Storey, Charles, Chartham, 123
Stoughton, Thomas, St. Martin's, 13
Stratford, Archbishop, 53, 59, 90
Strangford, Viscount, 147
Stukeley, Dr., 99
Sturry, 147
Sudbury, Archbishop, Westgate, 89, 97
Suppression of the Priories, 109
Swift, Dean, his ancestors rectors of St. Andrew's, 94
Taylor, Rev. Edward, Bifrons, 140
Teynham Lord, a descendant of the Ropers, 86, 147
Thanington, 113
Thorn, a monk of St. Augustine, 6, 17
Tonford Manor, remains of, 119
Tournament, at St. Stephen's, 79
Towers of the City Walls, 98
Trinity Chapel, St. Dunstan's, 87
Tumulus, at Iffin, 116; Chilham, 131
Twyne, John, St. Paul's, 76
Valoyns family, 116
Vicarage of Thanington, the ancient, 114
Waleys, Sir William, 116
Walls of the City, 96
Warham, Archbishop, 79, 111
Watson, John, St. Margaret's, 73
Weekes, Henry, R.A., of Canterbury, 70
Westgate, 102
Whitefriars, 104
Whitgift, Archbishop, Eastbridge, 62
Wido, Abbot, St. Augustine's, 25
Winter, John, St. Margaret's, 73
Wincheap Gate, 98
Woodall, Rev. E. H., St. Margaret's, 72
Workhouse, The old, 109
Worthgate, The, 98
Wotton, Lord, St. Augustine's, 26

www.ingramcontent.com/pod-product-compliance
Lightning Source LLC
Chambersburg PA
CBHW030246170426
43202CB00009B/644